MARCO  POLO

SIC ILY

T0166786

AUSTRIA
SLOVEN.
Milan Verona
ITALY
CROATIA
BOSN. &
HERZEG.
SAN
MARINO
SERBIA
MC
Corsica
(F)
Rome
MNE RK
S
ALBA-
NIA
Naples
Sardinia
(I)
Capri
*Mediterranean
Sea*
Palermo
Sicily

www.marco-polo.com

THE TOURING APP

shows you the way...
including routes and offline maps!

FREE!

GET MORE OUT OF YOUR MARCO POLO GUIDE

IT'S AS SIMPLE AS THIS

1 go.marco-polo.com/sic

2 download and discover

GO!

WORKS OFFLINE!

SYMBOLS

INSIDER TIP	Insider Tip
★	Highlight
⬤⬤⬤⬤	Best of...
☼	Scenic view
♲	Resonsible travel: for ecological and fair trade aspects

PRICE CATEGORIES HOTELS

Expensive   over 120 euros

Moderate   80–120 euros

Budget   under 80 euros

Prices for a double room with breakfast in the high season (except 1–20 August) per nIght

PRICE CATEGORIES RESTAURANTS

Expensive   over 40 euros

Moderate   25–40 euros

Budget   under 25 euros

Prices for a meal with starter, main course and dessert, without drinks and cover

CONTENTS

MAPS IN THE GUIDEBOOK
(136 A1) Page numbers and
coordinates refer to the road
atlas
(0) Site/address located off
the map. Coordinates are
also given for places that are
not marked on the road atlas

City map of Syracuse on p. 56

(🗺 A1) refers to the
removable pull-out map

INSIDE FRONT COVER:
The best Highlights

INSIDE BACK COVER:
City maps of Catania,
Palermo, Taormina and
Trapani

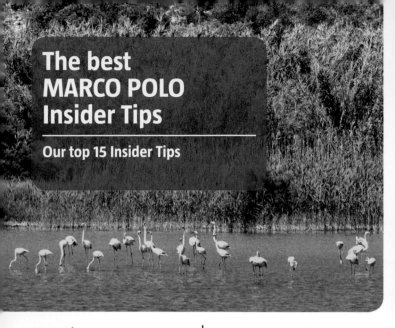

The best MARCO POLO Insider Tips

Our top 15 Insider Tips

INSIDER TIP ▶ Devils and Co.
On Good Friday in *San Fratello,* villains in red with masks and tin drums take to the streets and interrupt the processions. Priests and the police take no notice – and the crowds love it → **p. 120**

INSIDER TIP ▶ Pure bliss
In *Vendicari* Nature Reserve you can watch flamingos, herons and storks from close up, walk for miles along empty beaches without seeing anyone and explore a holiday paradise between sandbanks and lagoons (photo above) → **p. 53**

INSIDER TIP ▶ Return of the goddesses
Two ancient statues have returned to *Aidone* after their exile in America → **p. 50**

INSIDER TIP ▶ The impregnable
Sheer cliff faces, several defence walls and just one steep approach with heavily fortified gates made the *Rocca di Cefalù* impregnable. Paths now lead up to the top of the 268 m (880 ft) high rock above Cefalù although the best view of the Old Town and the cathedral is half way up (photo right) → **p. 62**

INSIDER TIP ▶ Lots of sand all to yourself
Dunes, woods, fine sand, clear water and few people make the beaches between *Sciacca* and *Montallegro* the perfect place to enjoy a peaceful day sunbathing, swimming or snorkelling → **p. 80**

INSIDER TIP ▶ A hidden paradise
The lush green *Gardens of the Kolymbetra* are hidden below the temples in Agrigento and cult sites of earthly gods. Their almond and orange trees have turned this into a true Garden of Eden → **p. 74**

INSIDER TIP ▶ Elegant trattoria
Pina Mandarano's fish recipes attract the Milanese fashionistas holidaying on *Panarea.* Remember to pre-book in summer! → **p. 94**

INSIDER TIP The gaze of the Madonna

Antonello da Messina's small "Annunciation" in the *Galleria Regionale della Sicilia* in Palermo is a great masterpiece → **p. 66**

INSIDER TIP Hiking among the palms

The *Riserva dello Zingaro* has enticing bays enclosed by cliffs, hiking paths above the coast and thousands of fan palm → **p. 85**

INSIDER TIP Swanky patisserie

Di Pasquale in Ragusa is a temple of *pasticceria siciliana,* selling the finest, world-class gateaux and petits fours → **p. 54**

INSIDER TIP Sicilian-style burgers

The tiniest start-up on Sicily: *Fud* is a mini chain of restaurants, operating two trendy establishments in Palermo and Catania, both open after midnight. Locals swear by the fantastic burgers made exclusively from Sicilian-reared organic beef → **p. 68**

INSIDER TIP An oriental dream

Arabian artists and builders created *La Zisa* castle – an elegant stone cube – in Palermo for the Norman rulers; its ingenious air-conditioning still works more than 800 years on → **p. 68**

INSIDER TIP Mamma Laura's recipes

Pasta with broad beans, twisted *busiate* pasta with pistachios or barbecued *castrato* mutton. Authentic Sicilian home-cooking at *M.A.T.E.S.* in Caltabellotta → **p. 80**

INSIDER TIP Sicilian icons

In his home town of Bagheria, the painter *Renato Guttuso* has left behind paintings full of melancholic *sicilianità*: prickly pear plants and hard-working fishermen → **p. 70**

INSIDER TIP B&B with vegetable garden

In her simple two-room guesthouse, *Signora Angelina* treats guests to delicious home-made *dolci* and limoncello → **p. 90**

BEST OF...

GREAT PLACES FOR FREE
Discover new places and save money

● **Tea-time**
You can find out everything to do with tea in the Feng-Shui-styled *Casa-Museo del Tè* in Raddusa. You can also have a cup, of course. Admission is free and, if you want to do some good, you can buy a small tea souvenir and support one of the Casa's charity projects → p. 51

● **With the eyes of the painter**
Two renditions of the city's patron saint, Lucia, are on exhibition for free (or for a small donation) at the chapel *Santa Lucia alla Badia:* One is the life-size silver sculpture with gouged-out eyes and the second is of the lying martyr painted in vivid light-dark colours in 1608 by Caravaggio, who had fled to Sicily because of murder → p. 58

● **Open-air gallery in a river valley**
Take a brisk walk rather than standing in a queue: the *Fiumara d'Arte*, with its large sculptures that can be seen from some distance, a pyramid and a labyrinth, is located on the hills above the Messina–Palermo coast road and in the rocky riverbeds → p. 62

● **Tapping the source**
Help yourself to mineral water directly from the spring – and free of charge – at the old *fountain* outside the mountain village of Geraci Siculo. Just take your own bottles to fill up and a bit of patience, as you'll have to wait your turn → p. 64

● **Throbbing street market**
Market criers, mutton heads, swordfishes, pepper-flavoured cheeses and piles of blood oranges: Palermo's busiest street market *Ballaró* is a fascinating mix of culinary delights at rock-bottom prices → p. 69

● **Column drums from Antiquity**
For over 2300 years, column drums intended for building temples in Selinunt have been lying in *Rocche di Cusa*. With your Selinunt ticket, you get a lovely free stroll in natural surroundings through Antiquity (photo) → p. 79

● *A cap with a history*

Once a symbol of the Mafia: the *coppola,* the Sicilian peaked cap made of hardwearing material. Fashion designers have rediscovered it. You can even find them in velvet – or in white to go with a wedding dress. Whatever your taste, head for *La Coppola Storta* in Palermo → p. 68

● *Puppet shows*

See wild fights and loud kisses in the marionette theatres *Vaccaro-Mauceri* in Syracuse and *Argento* in Palermo, where knights of old fight the Saracens or come to the rescue of damsels in distress. Great fun – and not just for children → p. 119

● *Intensive aromas*

Oregano and wild fennel make Sicilian dishes so tasty. The herbs used in local dishes on the Aeolian Islands produce the most intense aromas. Find out for yourself by sampling the delicious food in *Kasbah* on Lipari or in *Punta Lena* on Stromboli → p. 89, 93

● *Veg to go*

The real *caponata* made of aubergines, celery, capers, green olives, wild fennel and tomatoes is eaten cold. Farmers take it with them to the fields. Try this classic *cucina povera* at the trattoria *San Giovanni* in Gela → p. 76

● *Ceramic works of art*

The Arabs left their mark on Sicilian art: dazzling blues, delicate yellows, a little red – typical colours of the ceramics found in Caltagirone, Sciacca and Burgio (photo). You'll find particularly bright colours along the main road in *Santo Stefano di Camastra* → p. 63

● *Intoxicated by the colours and smells*

The *street markets* in Catania and Palermo with their colourful wares and bustling activity stimulate the senses. Immerse yourself in a world of artistically stacked fruit and vegetable pyramids, the variety of mysterious sea creatures on sale, the smell of fish and the scent of oranges. And even if you can't stomach the idea of a calf's foot decorated with myrtle twigs, then at least feast on the banquet with your eyes → p. 36, 68

ONLY IN

BEST OF...

● *Plates and bowls*
When it rains, the bright tiles on the walls of the *ceramics museum* in Caltagirone are especially lovely. Inside, the hundreds of tiles, vases, bowls, plates, jugs and figures from Antiquity until today are quite a sight – even when dry → p. 48

● *Archaeology under cover*
The mosaics in the Late Roman *Villa del Casale* near Piazza Armerina cover 44,130 ft² and have been roofed over. You can spend hours here looking at the excavations (photo) → p. 50

● *To the opera house for coffee*
Why not sip your cappuccino at the *Caffé del Teatro* at Palermo's *Teatro Massimo*? Italy's largest opera house includes magnificent decorations that you can marvel at in silence when the orchestra pit and stage are empty → p. 67

● *Sicilian cookery classes*
Take lessons in Sicilian cooking from an experienced signora who will teach you the best way to prepare classics such as maccheroni, involtini and *pasta alla norma*, for example at *Limoneto* near Siracusa or at *Agriturismo Gelso* in the Madonie Mountains → p. 19, 63, 124

● *Off to the spa*
Soak in the 38° C (100° F) warm spa water in *Terme Segestane* and you'll never notice that it's raining! Pure bliss in the evening after a long outing → p. 85

● *Spirit of wine*
Taste your way through orange liquors from Etna, the Nero d'Avola wines along the Cerasuolo di Vittoria wine route or the traditional Marsala wine from *Marco de Bartoli*. Meet new people, talk wines and enjoy the surroundings with *www.winerytastingsicily.com* → p. 77

RAIN

RELAX AND CHILL OUT
Take it easy and spoil yourself

● *Seeking refuge higher up*

In the stone-built *Azienda Agrituristica Cirasella* in Sant'Alfio, almost 3300 ft above sea level, you can enjoy the peace of a country holiday with just the sound of the birds below tall trees on the flanks of Mount Etna, and tuck into the excellent organic food produced on the farm → **p. 34**

● *Mountaineering made easy*

If you're not a keen hiker, then take a trip in the *cable car* up Etna (from the end of the road at Rifugio Sapienza) and soak up the magnificent views. For the remaining 9500 ft you can take a tour in an off-road minibus → **p. 37**

● *Boat trip through a green tunnel*

Sit back and enjoy a *boat trip* on the narrow, cool River *Ciane* south of Syracuse and marvel at the dense vegetation along the banks of reeds, couch grass and papyrus (photo) → **p. 59**

● *Oasis in the metropolis*

Stop off at the *botanic garden* in Palermo after a sightseeing trip – get away from the noise of the city. Sitting on a park bench under tropical trees and watching the rose-ringed parakeets from Africa flying among the treetops is pure relaxation → **p. 66**

● *An island of peace*

For those who really want to turn their backs on things, just take a boat from Salina to *Alicudi* and soak up the silence. A small harbour, a hotel and restaurant, a few houses on the main path to the top of the volcano – that's all there is on the island. Even the most active of people adopt a slower pace of life here → **p. 92**

● *Mineral massage*

Warm spring water fills the large pool in the *Terme di Acqua Pia* near Gibellina and you can experience its gentle power sitting under one of the waterfalls. Or else spoil yourself with a health and beauty therapy → **p. 78**

INTRODUCTION

DISCOVER SICILY!

"Araaaance, arance fresche dell'Etna!" Carmine the market crier's singsong echoes through the Baroque streets of Palermo's Old Town with its flaking façades – a drawn out falsetto like a plaintive Arab melody. Shutters are thrown open; widows dressed in black appear on balconies where canaries are kept in their cages. They lower their *paniere* – their wicker shopping baskets – on long ropes. The "Ape" three-wheeler van, with its colourful rusty patches, is piled high with blood oranges. The scent of the citrus fruit's leaves in the blazing summer heat mingles with the smell of swordfish in garlic from a *trattoria* with bright fluorescent lights and a flickering television. *Sicilia eterna* – the slow-paced "eternal" Sicily of old – really does still exist. But anyone who thinks that the few confusingly chaotic districts in the Old Town or the intoxicating hustle-and-bustle of the fish market are the real Sicily, is definitely behind the times.

Young student girls in tight jeans with jet-black hair down to their waists, sounding their horns on their Vespas with their "Mafia: no grazie" stickers, are neither "hot trophies" nor "token women", but simply part of everyday life. Their grandmothers, the older generation of *nonna*, used to be more hesitant about being out on the street, except when they went to church. An active lifestyle with cycling and hiking *(escur-*

More than 2400 years old – the Temple of Concorde in the Valle dei Templi near Agrigento

sionismo) has suddenly become hip among young Sicilians. Local groups put their new trekking shoes to the test in the *Riserva dello Zingaro* nature reserve in the far northeast, where their walks take them past abandoned tuna fisheries, swathes of yellow surge and turquoise bays. Renovated farms, now run as *agriturismi*, attract Italians from the north tired of the rat race as well as other Europeans who are into organic living. *Nero d'Avola* has turned into the local cult wine and top wine-makers refine the taste by completing the ripening process in clay amphoras.

> **Young Sicilians find cycling and hiking hip**

In the one real tourist hotspot on the island, in Taormina with its view of Etna photographed millions of times, five-star luxury hotels are sprouting up all over the place

800–580 BC
Founding of many Phoenician and Greek towns around the coast of Sicily

241 BC–468 AD
Sicily becomes a Roman province after the First Punic War and remains so for 700 years

827–1061
Sicily under Arab rule; Palermo becomes the capital city in 901

1061–91
Sicily is conquered by the Normans. A refined culture emerges during the 150 years under the Normans and the House of Hohenstaufen that combines Arabic, Byzantine and European traditions

like during the Belle Epoque. ... guests frequently include weeken... tors from larger cities, whereas durir... the lively and loud *movida* that ram-pages through Catania's lavic stone *centro storico* on balmy summer evenings, there are few holiday-makers to be found. Celebrations are more boisterous here than in the melancholic metropolis of Palermo. Provincial towns such as Comiso or Acireale have a surprising number of elegant boutiques. The typical man on Sicily today is dressed in a dark suit and tie – or else in a pink T-shirt as a *tifoso* of Palermo Calcio. For the first time in decades, a Sicilian football team is at last back in the first division.

The old picture of the hard-done-by south, always seeing itself as the exploited victim with little much to offer other than organised crime, a declining population and poverty, is a picture that no longer applies. *Vittimismo* as a frame of mind is now *passé*. Even the all-pavading Mafia has mutated into an economic driving force and an attraction for cineastes. Since the province of Palermo has been promoting its image at travel and tourism fairs with companies that refuse to pay the *pizzo* (protection money), the threat has boosted tourism: "We are anti Mafia" has turned into a tourist experience. The flat cap cap worn by tanned farm-workers and Sicilian gangsters has returned as a cheekily striped piece of Hollywood headgear. Even the *baristas* at the aiport wear their *coppola* with charming nonchalance.

Sicilia est insula: this truism drummed into the heads of Latin pupils conceals more than first meets the eye. Covering 25,709 km² (9927 sq miles) it is the largest island in the Mediterranean – and a very special one at that. It is closer to Libya and Tunisia than to Milan. And it is too powerful, too culturally important, too modern to pretend

1266
After the death of the Staufen king Frederick II, the Pope puts the French Anjou family on the throne of Sicily

1282–1700
Sicily comes under the rule of the Spanish crown

1734–1860
Under the rule of the Bourbons who also command Naples

1860
The conquest of Sicily by Garibaldi marks the start of the Unification of Italy

ca. 1870
The wave of emigration to America starts; ten years later the Mafia and organised crime take hold

...here provincial, Mediterranean outpost. The Ancient Greeks performed their ...mprovised comedies in Syracuse while the temples in Agrigento continue to ...vide a fascinating display of harmonious proportion. Carpaccio or sashimi: Star chefs from Trapani or Ragusa jet back and forth to Tokyo to let the Japanese in on the secrets of the *cucina siciliana*. Dolce donna mia... Whereas Italian once evolved into the language of literature at royal courts in central Europe, computer programmers and software engineers in Etna Valley today have long since had to come to grips with the niceties of English. After years of neglect, the Art Nouveau *Teatro Massimo* in Palermo resounds once again to the sound of Bellini, Wagner and Puccini. Young Sicilians flirt quite openly with their oriental cultural heritage – "Arab revival" is what they call it here – while TV cookery shows enthuse about the *cassata's* Islamic roots. In the long term, the political upheaval in Maghreb will provide Sicily with other possibilities then just taking in refugees on Lampedusa. The fishing centre and port of Mazara del Vallo would long since have stopped trading were it not for workers from Tunisia. However, the influx of war refugees and asylum seekers who attempt the dangerous crossing from North Africa continues to be a widely discussed problem throughout Europe.

> **The largest island in the Mediterranean is closer to Libya than Milan**

Un ponte sullo stretto – even without the controversial bridge across the strait between Messina and Reggio di Calabria, the more than 5 million Sicilians have been drawing ever closer to the rest of Europe. They have long become well integrated throughout mainland Italy as judges and poets, car mechanics and publicans, *carabinieri* and film directors. And yet Sicily still sometimes seems like a continent unto itself, running at a different pace and according to different rules. Even the colours are different. Everything somehow seems more intense. Nowhere else are the cherry trees and prickly pears, the cucumbers and aubergines as bright and shiny. In no other operatic performance is the public so vociferous as during *Cavalleria Rusticana*. Where else does the baleful music of Easter processions echo more sullenly through the mountain villages or do children, dressed as nuns and monks, drag along behind the decorated carts marking the Passion the evening before Good Friday? The Spanish and the Greeks, the Albanians and French, Normans and North Africans have all left their mark in the form of fortresses and cathedrals, sagas and culinary delights, mu-

1943–47
Mafia terror against land reform, the black market and separatists almost plunge Sicily into civil war

Since 1975
The Mafia blatantly terrorises the state. Resistance is slow to form. In 1993, the "Boss of Bosses", Totò Riina, is arrested, followed by his successor, Bernardo Provenzano, in 2006

2017
Sicily has become Europe's front line for refugees attempting the precarious crossing as *boat people* from North Africa

2018
Palermo is named Italy's Capital of Culture

The snowy-white "Stair of the Turks" juts out of the sea near Agrigento: Scala dei Turchi

sic and facial features. The island has been multicultural for thousands of years to which the mass of historical sights testify.

The luxuriant cascades of bougainvillea, the spikey orange cactus fruit and the silvery-grey olive and knarled carob trees of the coastal regions provide a stark contrast to the sulphury, seemingly uninhabited countryside further inland with its waving fields of corn, overgrown paths, flocks of sheep in the *macchia*. The variety of beaches is also quite considerable, ranging from fine sand along the north coast, such as the one framing the fishing town of Cefalù at the foot of the limestone Madonie mountains, to pebbly lava beaches on the Aeolian island of Lipari. With blue grottoes below Taormina and the Gola d'Alcantara volcanic gorge, all the delights of the south are concentrated on Sicily.

> **All the delights of the south are concentrated on Sicily**

Sicilians like being together with friends or engrossed in conversation, and – like Andrea Camilleri's Inspector Montalbano – enjoy long feasts. *La bella figura*, extravagant tips, demonstrative idleness and tireless commentaries and appraisals with erotic undertones are eternal traits of the *sicilianità*, as is the joy at meeting new people – demonstrated sometimes just a little bit too fast. The friend that Carmine the orange seller wanted to photograph suddenly finds herself surrounded by a number of other photo models – *anche a me* "why not me as well," says Rosario, the gaunt owner of the trattoria opposite, as he forces himself into the picture, proudly holding up a tray of *cannoli* filled with fruit and ricotta...

1 Modern architecture

In with the new Once over, Sicily only looked to restore its crumbling Baroque architecture and it took an earthquake like the Gibellina earthquake in 1968 to build new buildings. This has changed now. International architecture magazines praise constructions such as the *Ecò-Bar (Via Mariano Rumor 40)*, which Giuseppe Gurrieri created by converting the old ticket office of a sports arena or the amazing *Specus corallii* grotto *(Via Generale Domenico Giglio 12)* by Antonio Cardillo in Trapani, which is opened for concerts. Also attracting attention are boutique hotels like the *Caol Ishka (Via Elorina 154 | www.caolishka. it)* in Syracuse which combines minimalistic lines with Bourbon decorative elements.

2

Natural beauty

Looking lovely Salt, olive oil and lemons: local products are put to good use in the spa in the *Kempinski Hotel Giardino di Costanza (Via Salemi km 7 | Mazara del Vallo) (photo)*. The cosmetics industry makes use of Sicily's fragrances as well: Dolce & Gabbana created their "Sicily" perfume with top notes of bergamot. *Ortigia Profumi* runs shops on the island as well as in London, Florence and Berlin selling prickly pear bath oils in big cat flacons.

3 Highlife on the beach

Night and day The beach clubs are only empty in the mornings when clearing up after the previous night is underway. The cool clubs acts as a magnet however long before sunset. *Paradise Beach Club (Via Luigi Rizzo | Letoianni) (photo)* starts off as a relaxing lounge bar then becomes an elegant restaurant before turning into a disco after dark. Samuele offers a more casual daytime venue at the intimate *Puerto*

There are lots of new things to discover on Sicily. A few of the most interesting are listed below

Rico Beach Club (Via Nazionale 140 | Villagonia), accessible through a pedestrian tunnel near the train station at Taormina.

Green lodgings

4

Where the lemon trees blossom ● The protection of the environment is a topic chiefly embraced by the *agriturismo* farms. Organic is spelt with a capital "O" on the lemon farm ● *Limoneto (Via del Platano 3 | Syracuse | www.limoneto. it) (photo)*, also in the kitchen where you can sample the delights of the Sicilian cuisine. Cooking on solar power and showing with rainwater: the *Etnalodge (Via Bassi 21 | Piedimonte Etneo | www.etnalodge.it)* shows, also in workshops, how to save energy at home. At *Agriturismo Guarnera (Collesano | www.guarnera.it)*, even the pool is fitted with a natural chlorine-free filtration system.

The South's take on ice cream

5

Gelato artigianale ● The Sicilians copied their recipe for ice cream from the Arabs: They harvested snow from Mount Etna to cool their fruit juices and almond pastes rather than using milk and cream as in the North. Islanders prefer eating ice-cold breakfasts during the hot summer months. *Granita* is the magic word, a sorbet served in a variety of unusual flavours such as mulberries *(photo)*, prickly pear or roasted almonds. Newer *gelatieri* like *Gelati Divini (cathedral square)* in Ragusa compete for customers with aromas such as carob bean, blood orange or Marsala while the "old hand" *Costanzo (Via Spaventa 7)* in Noto creates fantastic mandarin and jasmine sorbets which would melt anyone's taste buds.

IN A NUTSHELL

BURDENS OF THE PAST & HOPEFUL GREENS

Even travellers in the18th century commented on the rubbish in Palermo. Since time immemorial Sicilians have treated the environment with typical Mediterranean *laissez-faire*. Industrial ruins, concrete eyesores and (although decreasing in number) illegal dumps are the downside of *bella Sicilia*.

However there has been a noticeable rethink. The Regional Agency for the Protection of the Environment (ARPA) campaigns in schools, boats patrol the coasts to make sure there is no illegal building work. The regional parks and more than 50 conservation areas are visited by enthusiastic local hikers or *escursionisti*. The number of *bandiera blu* beaches (with a blue flag for ecological awareness) still has to be expanded. *Mangiare sano:* the considerable value now placed on health food has resulted in Italian's sun-blessed island becoming the biggest supplier of organic products. The younger generation is well aware as to how the economy of post-industrial Sicily can only benefit from an ecologically "green" image. Sicily has emerged as a stronghold of the slow-food movement with an abundance of regional restaurants and eateries embracing the values of "good, clean, fair" and "traditional, regional" stipulated by the definitive guide of good food in Italy, the "Osterie d'Italia". The mass of fish in the markets rather hides the fact that tuna is acutely endangered – something, how-

Addio pizzo, ciao coppola: Sicily between the Mafia and hip headgear, boat people and organic fare, the Church and the *corso*

ever, that is more due to fleets of sea-going vessels than Sicilian fishing boats.

COPPOLA & CO.

The *coppola*, the flat cap, now enjoys cult status and is a fashionable expression of *sicilianità* – quite independent of a person's social status. It used to be common for men in the country to wear flat caps as it indicated that they were tenant farmers, agricultural workers, peasants or shepherds. More sturdy hats with a wider brim were reserved for the rural and provincial bourgeoisie and the nobility. The *coppola* got a bad name through its association with the Mafia as it was largely worn by the big bosses' right-hand men. But in the meanwhile even Hollywood stars like Brad Pitt can be seen in a *coppola*. And a leading Sicilian hat-maker has opened up shops in New York and Berlin *(www.lacoppolastorta.it)*.

HONOURABLE SOCIETY

The Mafia, the Godfathers and their killers have a hand in virtually everything that has to do with power and money. Drugs and prostitution, the smuggling of refugees and the extortion of protection money are just the openly criminal activities. A network of friendships with politicians and officials right up to the top opens up the path to big money for public contracts and subventions, creates minor posts and furthers major careers. The Mafia is a parallel state whose instruments of power include corruption, fear and murder. Whoever breaks the *omertà*, the pledge of secrecy, pays for it with his life. The internal power struggles are equally lethal, with most deaths coming from within the Mafia's own ranks whenever new bosses and families fight for their share.

The modern Mafia in major cities has long been operating on a global scale, networking both legal and criminal businesses especially in the road construction and the health industries, as well as in waste disposal. The annual turnover is estimated at up to 140 billion euros! Such capital is increasingly being invested in legal businesses, often in the form of hostile takeovers.

Those who bravely stand up to the Mafia still risk being killed. Murders are becoming increasingly brutal, not even stopping short of children. However, the success had in searching for the perpetrators and the severe sentences without reprieve, combined with the solidarity and increased self-confidence of the general public, have weakened the Mafia. And instead of sitting in silence for the rest of their lives in prison, many of the "bosses" spill the beans. The 'Ndrangheta clans in Calabria have long gained an altogether more brutal reputation than their relatively "civilized" counterparts in Sicily, despite their cinematic representation.

This new image fits in with the island's political sensation, created by the homosexual anti-mafia activist and left-wing politician Rosario Crocetta who was voted to become President of the Sicilian region for the term 2012–2017. Confiscated property and the businesses of convicted bosses are made over to cooperatives and also provide a glimmer of hope, helping to ease the state of permanent unemployment in the countryside. They produce pasta, oil, cheese and wine under the trademark "Libera Terra" *(www.libera terra.it)*. The cooperatives themselves have joined forces with hoteliers, traders, farmers, craftsmen and builders – more than 800 in total –to form "Addio Pizzo" and no longer pay protection money *(pizzo)*. A map with all addresses – largely in the city and province of Palermo – is available wherever you see the "Addio Pizzo" sticker on the door or under *www.addio pizzo.org*. For Catania and the Etna region see *www.addiopizzocatania.org*.

L'ISOLA DELLA MUSICA

Sounds reverberate around this island where the singer Caruso once made his name; ranging from the Easter procession brass bands, the verismo opera "Cavalleria Rusticana" (known even to implacable Opera haters from the film "Godfather III") or even a siciliano in E-flat major from Johann Sebastian Bach. However, the island is not dogged in musical tradition even though the young generation is frantically discovering the island's folkloric heritage, mixed with jazz or Latin American influences. In particular, the melancholic Fado-influenced songs by Rosa Balistreri (1927–90) enjoy a cult following: The "Sicilian Edith Piaf" grew up in the poorest conditions which made her ballades so authentic. New Sicilian stars have now taken to the stage such as the songwriter Carmen Consoli, the rock legend Franco Battiato, the musician Luca Madonia or Ivan Segret●

who specialises in lounge music in dialect. The *Zanne Festival (www.zannefestival.com)* held in Catania is a symbiosis of world music and the Sicilian music scene. And where else in Europe will you find so many hotels and night clubs

km/86 miles off the Tunisian coast. The inflatable boats are often overcrowded and in miserable conditions, causing the drowning of hundreds of travellers. Italy and Sicilian fishermen who have been rescuing those stranded and in distress

The *cantautrice* Carmen Consoli is on a par with rock legends such as Gianna Nannini

with piano bars where real-life pianists perform live?!

MEDITERRANEAN FATALITIES

From an EU perspective, Sicily, the island at the heart of the Mediterranean, used to hold a border post perched on the edge of Europe. However this has now changed. Tens of thousands of refugees, who make the perilous boat crossing from Libya and Tunisia to Europe in the hope of escaping the desperate conditions in Africa, have become the subject of heavy political discussion. Not only desperate boat people from Africa but also Syrian and Afghan refugees fleeing civil war attempt to reach Lampedusa by boat, which is located just 138

for years feel abandoned by the EU in terms of the marooned beaches and the number of refugees. Lampedusa alone has witnessed a serious slump in tourism as a result of the refugee camps and the horrific possibility of drowned refugees being washed ashore. It remains to be seen whether the EU plans for migrant processing centres in North Africa will help to curb the flow of people.

OFF WITH THEIR HEADS!

Heads roll, Saracens are split in two and princesses abducted. There's never a dull moment in Sicilian marionette theatres, the *Opera dei Pupi*, when Orlando or Reynald fight for the Cross or for Charlemagne. But even the *puparo*, the puppeteer, can get out of breath, as performing is hard physical work in these family-run businesses. The brightly-coloured figures can be up to 1½ m (5 ft) high. They are hand-carved and operated using iron rods. In the 1980s this form of folk art was in danger of disappearing due to dwindling audiences. Now, however, even local school classes now visit the shows. Palermo, Acireale and Syracuse are the principle centres on Sicily where shows are held (see p. 119). In 2008 the Opera dei Pupi *(www.pupisiciliani.com)* was designated by Unesco as part of humanity's "oral and intangible heritage".

SARACEN TOWERS

The sturdy, sometimes round, sometimes square towers are a feature of the Italian coastline and also of Sicily. The Saracens from north Africa arrived on the shores of all Christian countries around the Mediterranean in the 9th century in their ships, plundered and destroyed coastal settlements and fought their way into the heart of the country, killing the local populace or taking them back for the slave market. Well fortified towns, however, were seldom attacked. The towers were within sight of one another and warnings were given by lighting fires or firing canons. This permanent feud lasted until the start of the 19th century; most of the Saracen towers are Spanish fortresses from the 16th century. Today, many of the towers have been converted into hotels or discos.

SICILIA SANTA

Almost all Sicilians are Catholic. The Church still has a strong influence on virtually all aspects of everyday life and always makes itself heard, even if it has to apply a little pressure. The majority of kindergartens and a lot of schools are in the hands of the Church, as are many social institutions. The influence of nuns on children and mothers is widespread even if the involvement of the Church is only apparent outwardly. Marrying in white and a church funeral are a matter of course; regular church attendance less so. Women are definitely more active in this respect – with this involvement increasing with age. Church groups, priests, members of religious orders and church dignitaries are working more and more for changes. Answers to the problem of the Mafia and people's fear of it, building and land speculation, corruption in politics, the decimation of the environment, spiralling drug addiction and petty criminality in urban centres, unemployment and a renewed increase in illiteracy, are often sought in the Church.

STROLLING & FLIRTING

The *passeggiata* – the evening stroll – starts before the sun has set. Everyone seems to be on the move and the main thoroughfare, the *corso*, as well as the main square, the *piazza*, are turned into a stage for two hours, where people meet up and like to see and be seen by friends and anyone around. Gossip and news are exchanged and rumours spread. The *passeggiata* is also the perfect, carefully monitored occasion for lovers to show their affection for one another. This is when many an engagement and marriage finds its beginnnings and business deals are settled.

TRINACRIA

The winged woman's head with the two serpents, from which three legs emerge, has been used as an emblem for Sicily since Antiquity, symbolising its triangular shape and its three ancient provinces, as well as being a symbol of the sun and of fertility. Sicily's emblem can be seen everywhere – on postcards and souvenirs, on market stalls, fishing boats and lorries, on pub and shop signs, as a trademark o a brewery in Messina, on stamps, flags, Internet sites and official letterheads.

VOLCANOES & EARTHQUAKES

Geologically speaking, most of Sicily was part of Africa. Only the north is part of the Eurasian Plate and is being pushed by the African Plate which resulted in the formation of the mountain ranges in northern Sicily. Earthquakes are caused by tension and the sudden release of energy in the earth's crust. In 1693, a quake destroyed the whole of southern Sicily. In 1783 and 1908 the most devastating earthquakes ever recorded in Europe almost entirely destroyed Messina; in 1969 it hit Gibellina in the west and 13 other settlements in Belice Valley.

Volcanoes often appear along the seams where cracks and faults cause chambers of magma – which rise from the molten centre of the earth – to form. Etna and Stromboli are the two most visibly active volcanoes on Sicily. For volcanologists, the islands of Lipari, Vulcano, Panarea and Pantelleria are still active, although their last eruptions were more than 100 years ago. The islands Salina, Filicudi, Alicudi, Ustica and Linosa are extinct volcanoes.

Off the coast of Sicily, deep under the sea, there is a lot more going on. In the very shallow waters to the south, which are rich fishing grounds, between Agrigento, Sciacca, Pantelleria and Linosa, fisherman frequently find cooked fish in their haul and they see air bubbles rising. Deep under the Tyrrhenian Sea, north of the Aeolian Islands, lies Europe's largest, active volcanoe, Marsili, that covers an area of more than 770 sq miles and rises to a height of some 3000 m (9850 ft). It is still relatively poorly researched and surrounded by a ring of craters including at least seven other active, underwater volcanoes and the Aeolian Islands above the water. Marsili is permanently under surveillance. It cannot be predicted if and when it will erupt or cause an undersea earthquake with a devastating tsunami.

Even grandmas don't like missing out on the evening *passeggiata* in Taormina

FOOD & DRINK

Forget the picture you have of typical Italian food, of spaghetti bolognese and *frittura*. Sicilian cuisine is different. It's made up of the culinary delights enjoyed by all foreign rulers who made the island their home for hundreds of years.

The food is different on every part of the island. Fishermen and shepherds, farmers from the fertile plains and workers from the great expanse of inland Sicily all have different ingredients at hand. And the food of the gentry is different again from that of their staff. But what they do have in common is creativity, fantasy and a love of colour, as well as an ability to combine sweet, savoury, hot and sour things quite daringly which, in the hands of Sicilian cooks, are magically turned into delicious dishes. Fresh white bread, usually with

sesame seeds in the oriental tradition, and the omnipresent *pasta* are never missing. The Sicilians are even record-holders within Italy, consuming more than 100 kg of pasta per capita every year. The other main ingredients in traditional Sicilian food are as varied as an average market stall. *Seafood* and *vegetables* are essential; oregano and wild fennel, that can be found everywhere in Sicily, are used together with generous quantities of fresh mint from the garden and basil.

The Sicilians eat late, both at lunchtime and in the evening. And they like eating, especially in a restaurant. They also have a good time on a Sunday picnic in the woods, the mountains or on the beach. Eating is a pleasure spending a relaxing time with friends. A generous sandwich – *panino* –

Seafood, pasta and vegetables are the staple ingredients – regardless of whether you try the cuisine of fishermen or that of barons

or something fried such as rice balls – *ran-cini* – or chickpea biscuits – *panelli* – soon fill you up. Eating out in a restaurant normally starts with *antipasti*, small delicious appetisers which tempt the eye and tease the taste buds, and which Italians seldom skip. They include seafood, mushrooms, olives, cooked or marinated vegetables, local cheeses, hams and salami, and perhaps chilled melon or fresh figs. The *peimo piatto*, the first course, is almost always a noodle dish, but could equally well be risotto or a plate of *gnoc-chetti*, marble sized potato balls served with a light tomato sauce. *Cuscus alla trapanese*, the steamed wheat dish, is of north-African origin and is served with a hot fish soup.

The *secondo piatto* is the main course of seafood, meat or eggs. This is usually accompanied by a side dish *(contorno)* which has to be ordered separately, comprising a salad or cooked vegetables that are often eaten cold in Sicily. The Strait of Messina and the north coast between Cefalù and the Aeolian Islands are in sum-

LOCAL SPECIALITIES

alici marinate – marinaded anchovies with fresh mint

arancine – savoury-filled rice balls, coated with bread crumbs and deep fried

cannoli – small, crisp pasta rolls with a creamy ricotta filling (photo left)

caponata – sweet-and-sour aubergines served cold with tomatoes, olives, capers and herbs

cicorie selvatiche – wild greens (e.g. dandelion, rocket, thistle, fennel), usually rather bitter and acerbic

coniglio al agrodolce – sweet-and-sour marinaded rabbit

farsumagru – large veal roulade (700–800 g) filled with meat, eggs, olives, breadcrumbs and herbs

insalata di arance – fresh oranges with delicately-tasting onions and olive oil

insalata di mare – seafood in an olive oil and lemon marinade (photo right)

maccheroni alla Norma – homemade pasta with fresh tomato sauce, grilled slices of aubergine and fresh or smoked ricotta

maccu di fave – broadbean purée with olive oil and wild herbs

olive fritte – black olives braised with garlic and herbs

pani cunzatu – farmhouse bread filled with tomatoes, capers, olives, grated cheese, oregano and olive oil

parmigiana di melanzane – casserole with aubergines, tomatoes, Parmesan and mozzarella

pasta con finocchio e sarde – pasta with wild fennel and fresh sardines

peperonata – oven-baked peppers in oil and vinegar marinade

pesto trapanese – red tomato sauce with roasted almonds

sarde a beccafico – roulade filled with deboned sardines, in Palermo with breadcrumbs, sultanas and pine nuts baked in the oven, or in the east with breadcrumbs, Pecorino and anchovies cooked in a pan

spaghetti/risotto col nero di seppia – spaghetti or risotto with octopus in its own ink

tagliatelle con ragù di maiale – spicey hot tagliatelle with pork ragout

tonno alla marinara – with onions, olives, capers and tuna braised in tomatoes

zuppa di pesce – fish soup with 4–5 different types of fish, small squid and shrimps; sometimes also with mussels and scampi

mer the best fishing grounds in Italy for swordfish. Its lean meat is cooked on a charcoal grill, steamed with sweet tomatoes, capers and herbs or served with an olive oil, lemon, garlic and oregano sauce *(pesce spada al sammurighiu)*. Inland, the cuisine is dominated by lamb, rabbit, chicken and the coarse Sicilian sausage, the *salsiccia* (made only of pork mixed with fennel seeds, pepper and a little white wine to taste).

Sicilians often like to round off the meal with a dessert, normally with fruit of the season. On more special occasions, a *dolce* is served, such as a light almond cake often soaked in liqueur. The famous *martorana* – perfectly shaped pieces of fruit made of marzipan – are usually only for decoration.

The Sicilians see themselves as the inventors of ice cream. Even back in the 19th century, the snow on Etna was used as a natural cooling agent and was taken to the towns packed under masses of straw where it was kept in caves and cellars. Sicilian fruit ice cream is always made using fresh fruit. Wild strawberry ice cream is particularly popular. The *granita* is a semi-frozen crystalline dessert made with fruit pulp, almond milk or espresso and is particularly refreshing.

Wine production in Sicily has conquered the global market. Since wine growers have started harvesting grapes earlier, the red and white wines are dry with a good bouquet and – the white wines especially – are light and sparkling. In terms of wine, the island is divided into two: red wines dominate the eastern half, the *Nero d'Avola* grape having been rediscovered more recently. The most important wine-producing areas are in the southeast and on the northern and eastern flanks of Mount Etna with their fashionable *orange wines*. The western half is definitely a white wine region. The principal regions are the Jato and Belice valleys as well as the plains near Marsala where good dessert wines are produced.

Apart from wine, the most important drink for the Sicilians is water. Almond milk *(latte di mandorla)* and freshly pressed orange or lemon juice are also absolutely delicious. And every Sicilian is happy to join friends for a quick *caffè* at a bar at any time.

Delicious almond biscuits: Merletti di Mandorle

SHOPPING

Craftwork has a long tradition in Sicily and still dominates many towns. Although many craftsmen have disappeared from the everyday scene, such as tailors, cobblers and basket weavers, Sicily's ceramicists, marionette carvers and rug makers are highly productive. Demand is rising – Sicilians themselves have also rediscovered the crafts produced on their island. Good pieces are not always easy to find and have their price, and you'll be unlikely to find a bargain – this also goes for the antiquity shops. And then of course there is the imported touristy kitsch.

CERAMICS

Imaginative shapes and bright glazes have always found expression in Sicily's ceramics. Good and top quality pieces can still be found in Caltagirone, Burgio, Sciacca and Santo Stefano di Camastra. The majority of ceramics – bright, glazed majolica tiles, terracotta figures or models of Sicilian carts – are based on Arabian and Spanish pieces.

CORAL & JEWELLERY

Trapani was once famous throughout the whole Mediterranean for its coral products. This has virtually disappeared today since the coral reefs off the west coast of Sicily have been entirely decimated and the coral workshops in Torre del Greco near Naples have claimed the coral trade for themselves. Apart from a lot of gaudy merchandise, the *vu cumprà*, hawkers on beaches, also have a few good things, such as jewellery made of silver thread, shells and brightly-coloured pearls.

FASHION & DESIGN

To discover Sicilian design and fashion in the style of native fashion designer Marella Ferrera, simply follow the local, style-conscious signoras to the elegant streets near the Via Etnea in Catania and around the Via Libertá in Palermo. And of course – although usually much more expensive – in the boutiques in Taormina and on Lipari. The markets are awash with cheap goods and fakes of brand names. Or alternatively you dress from head to toe in pink and out yourself as a fan of the local US Palermo football club. Fashion victims can hunt for bargains from the half-Sicilian fashion label Dolce & Gabbana (Domenico Dolce originates from Madonie) at the *Sicilia Fashion Village* (see p. 50).

Majolica, Marsala or marionettes?
When buying souvenirs keep an eye out for quality and hand-crafted Sicilian products

FOOD

Sicily belongs to the south of Italy, which supplies Europe's markets with excellent 🌍 agricultural organic products. The chief products are (durum) wheat, wine, olive oil, almonds and citrus fruit – way over half of Italy's lemons and oranges are grown in the region. Sicily's wine production is also quite considerable both in quanity and quality. Many wineries have moved away from the traditional, heavy and potent wines of the past to the production of light, aromatic wines. Cheese producers *(caseificio)* inland and the small sausage manufacturers *(salumificio)* in the Nebrodi mountains and the high plateau region in the province of Ragusa, will gladly vacuum-pack their cheeses – made from sheep's, cow's or goat's milk – and their meat products. Gourmet souvenirs include elegantly packaged sea salt from the salt works of Trapani, expensive sardine glasses and tuna fish tins, mullet roe which is grated over pasta as dried *bottarga* as well as Europe's finest pistachios farmed in the Mount Etna region of Bronte, and last but not least marzipan.

MARIONETTES

Sicilian marionettes, made from wood, are well known. But even they are being mass produced now and Charlemagne can be found in all sorts of different variations. Original, second-hand marionettes are sometimes to be found at the puppet theatres in Acireale, Monreale and Palermo.

WOVEN ITEMS

Fan palms grow in the far west of the island and their fronds are used to make fashionable, light and beautiful bags, mats and hats. You'll find these in Scopello and San Vito lo Capo.

THE NORTHEAST

The Peloritani Mountains rise directly behind the narrow coastal strip. The ridge is covered by thick forest in many places, whereas the lower slopes are densely populated garden landscape.

One village runs into the next down the length of the coast. To the north are the seven Aeolian Islands. South of the mouth of the Alcantara, Mount Etna, Europe's highest active volcano, boasts the whole range of climate zones and vegetation that Sicily has to offer. Despite the catastrophes caused by eruptions, its flanks are densely populated. Breath-taking scenery, art and archeology, beaches, holiday centres such as Acireale and Taormina – everything in the northeast of Sicily is close together.

ACIREALE

(143 E1) (*∅ K5*) Acireale (pop. 53,000), together with its neighbouring villages, lies on an elevated lava terrace above the Ionian Sea, embedded among countless lemon groves whose green leafy roof is overshadowed by high palm trees.

The Baroque city owes its wealth to the lemon trade and the medicinal springs that have been used since Antiquity. Impressive façades line the main streets and squares. Experience life in the city on one of the three main interconnecting squares and enjoy looking at the town hall, the cathedral and the Baroque churches. A pretty street market can be visited in the mornings in the streets behind.

Peaks, gorges, beaches and a lively urban scene – that's Sicily in all its variety. And above all of this towers Mount Etna

FOOD & DRINK

LA GROTTA
Fish restaurant in a cavern in Santa Maria La Scala. *Closed Tue | Via Scalo Grande 46 | tel. 09 57 64 81 53 | Moderate–Expensive*

BEACHES

Most beaches are of the pebbly or rocky variety with few sandy stretches. The main places for swimming are the fishing villages *Santa Tecla* and *Santa Maria La Scala*.

ENTERTAINMENT

The *marionette theatre* in Acireale has a long tradition. The Grasso family puts on a great spectacle at its *Opera dei Pupi Turi Grasso (Via Naz. Per Catania | tel. 09 57 64 80 35 | www.operadeipupi. com)*.

WHERE TO STAY

Family-run hotels can be found mostly in the villages slightly higher up Etna.

Sit and chat on Piazza Duomo in Acireale

ACI E GALATEA

19th century style furnished hotel directly in the town centre. With guest fridge, WiFi and terrace. *3 rooms | Via San Carlo 22 | mobile tel. 33 85 61 93 86 | www.aciegalatea.it | Budget*

AGRITURISMO IL LIMONETO ✁

Located in *Scillichenti* above the cliffs with a garden and view of the sea and Etna. *5 flats | Via d'Amico 41 | tel. 0 95 88 65 68 | www.illimoneto.it | Budget*

INFORMATION

Servizio Turistico Regionale (Via Oreste Scionti 15 | tel. 0 95 89 19 99 | www.acire aleturismo.com)

WHERE TO GO

SANT'ALFIO (143 E1) (*⌖ K4*)

This mountain village on Mount Etna, 23 km (14 miles) to the north of Acireale, is well known for its cherries. Sicily's largest tree, the *Centocavalli*, a sweet chestnut estimated to be 1200 years old, can be found on the road to Milo. You can eat well in the restaurant at the organically-run ● ⊗ INSIDER TIP *Azienda Agrituristica Cirasella (4 flats | tel. 0 95 96 80 00 | www.cirasellaetna.it | Budget) nearby.*

ZAFFERANA ETNEA (143 D1) (*⌖ K5*)

21 km (13 miles) from Acireale, below the awe-inspiring volcanic Valle del Bove, lies this village, surrounded by gardens and chestnut woods. It is a popular tourist centre due to its healthy climate and good cuisine. INSIDER TIP *Caffè Donna Peppina* on the central Piazza Umberto is well known for its delicious pastries. If you prefer something more substantial try the puff pastry filled with cheese, anchovies or olives. Pleasant, family-run, medium standard hotels include *Primavera dell'Etna (57 rooms | tel. 09 57 08 23 48 | www.hotel-primavera.it | Budget–Moderate)*, in the middle of an olive grove, and the wellness hotel *Airone (62 rooms | tel. 09 57 08 18 19 | www.hotel-airone.it | Moderate–Expensive)*, above the village on the road to Rifugio Sapienza. Both serve very good plain food. ⊗ *Fermata Spuligni (Via Matteotti 1 | tel. 09 57 08 36 25 | www.fermataspuligni.com | Budget)*, a lovingly restored farmhouse with a pizzeria *(Tue–Sat evenings, Sun also lunch)*, is the perfect place to stay. Its 10 rooms are furnished with fairtrade pieces and textiles.

CATANIA

▨ **MAP INSIDE BACK COVER**
▨ (143 D2) (*⌖ K5*)) Chaotic, volcanic, seductive – Catania not only serves as a stopover to reach the island's beaches. With its own enigmatic charm

WHERE TO START?

Port: Parking spaces are few and far between so look for one near the port (Porto, Via/Piazza Alcala). From here, it's just a short walk to the cathedral and the fish market. Buses nos. 1–4 and 431 N run to the centre from the station. Long-distance coaches depart from the square in front of the station and from the streets nearby.

Sicily's second biggest city (pop. 313,000) is also known as *La Nera*, "the black city" due to Mount Etna, a powerful presence in Catania.

The architectonic ensemble of lava and basalt palazzi not only appeals to Baroque lovers – the city was completely redesigned by architects after the eruption of Etna in 1669 and the earthquake of 1693. The straight-as-a-die *Via Etnea* is lined with department stores selling fashion made in Sicily and ice-cream parlours serving the famous *granita*.

Catania, the university city with its North African climate, goes to bed late. The student crowd heads from the horse steak pubs near *Castello Ursino* to the pubs around the *Teatro Bellini* opera house. A more frenzied location is the city's morning market, just a few steps away from the Cathedral with its variety of colours, fruits, fish, noise and bustle, the close proximity of waste and picturesque market stalls, smells and aromas from its century-old multicultural cuisine. This is the pulsating heart of Sicily!

SIGHTSEEING

CASTELLO URSINO
The castle, constructed of black blocks of lava and with four massive corner towers,

is Catania's most distinctive medieval building. In 1669, it became surrounded by streams of lava. It now houses the *Museo Civico* with a picture gallery, collections of antiques, weapons and ceramics, as well as views of Mount Etna and ambitious special exhibitions. *Daily 9am–7pm | Piazza Federico II di Svevia | admission 6 euros*

CATANIA LIVING LAB
The Antiquity monuments of this Etna city reanimated in 3D. An experience not just for kids and computer fans. *Mon, Wed, Fri 9am–12.30pm | free admission | Via Manzoni 91 | www.catanialivinglab.it*

PIAZZA DUOMO
Cathedral Square with the black lava elephant is the central hub of the city, with the main shopping streets branching off

⭐ **Fish market**
Sicily's prettiest market is in Catania → p. 36

⭐ **Etna**
The largest active volcano in Europe → p. 37

⭐ **Ferrovia Circumetnea**
Round Mount Etna on the narrow gauge railway → p. 39

⭐ **Tindari**
Wonderful view of Lipari → p. 42

⭐ **Teatro Greco-Romano**
A view to die for: Mount Etna and the sea in Taormina → p. 44

⭐ **Alcantara Gorge**
Impressive testimony to the power of water → p. 45

MARCO POLO HIGHLIGHTS

Porta Uzeda is just ...quare is surround-...que town palaces of ... and church leaders. The ...drale di Sant'Agata is dedicated to St Agatha, the patron saint of Catania, whose reliquary is housed here. A fresco in the sacristy depicts the eruption of Etna in 1669.

TEATRO BELLINI
The interior of this magnificent building boasts ornate plasterwork, gold, red velvet and huge history paintings. It was inaugurated in 1890 with the Bellini opera "Norma".

VIA CROCIFERI
This street of palaces and churches with hotspots of student nightlife runs parallel to the Via Etnea, passing villas surrounded by small parks, to the university.

VILLA BELLINI ☆
The park in this district of 19th-century houses is named after the opera composer Vincenzo Bellini ("Norma"), who came from Catania. It contains busts of major Sicilian figures as well as an Art Nouveau music pavilion and good views.

FOOD & DRINK

Catania's cooking fuses Sicilian fish dishes with colourful vegetable platters, cheeses and mushrooms from Mount Etna. The city is famous for its *granita*, made by the big confectioneries along the Via Etnea, containing mulberries, lime juice or almond milk cooled with water ice.

OSTERIA ANTICA MARINA
In the heart of the *pescheria* district where the morning market thrives. Seafood in all its varieties, even Japanese. *Closed Wed | Via Pardo 29 | tel. 0 95 34 81 97 | www.anticamarina.it | Moderate*

SHOPPING

You should definitely find time for a stroll through Catania's ★ ● *fish market* at the *Porta Uzeda* in the *pescheria* district. It is Sicily's liveliest and most beautiful market which doesn't just sell fish, but all foods you can think of and all the fruit of Mount Etna. Don't forget, while you're being distracted by all the colours, smells and sounds, pickpockets like being in the thick of things too.

ENTERTAINMENT

ETOILE D'OR
Stylish bar with a bustling, interesting crowd of drinkers opened 24x7; its INSIDER TIP *tavola calda* offers a wide selection of snacks. *Closed Sun | Via Dusmet 7 | tel. 0 95 34 01 35 | Budget*

INSIDER TIP FIRST
Urban gardening, vibrant furniture, craft beers, graffiti and an olive tree in the red-light district of S. Berillo. A hotspot for local party-goers. *Daily 6pm–2am | Piazza delle Belle*

WHERE TO STAY

PALAZZU STIDDA
Stay in a sculptor's home at this family-friendly B&B right in the old town. *3 rooms | Vicolo della Lanterna 5 | mobile tel. 33 86 50 51 33 | www.palazzu-stidda. com | Budget*

VILLA PARADISO
Art Nouveau villa furnished in the style of the period with a garden and pool, view of the city, private beach. *30 rooms | in San Giovanni della Punta on the Viagrande*

Etna road (8 km/5 miles) | tel. 09 57 51 24 09 | www.paradisoetna.it | Expensive

Bureau del Turismo (Via Vittorio Emanuele 172 | tel. 09 57 42 55 73 | www.comune. catania.it) and *Servizio Turistico Regionale (Via Beato Bernardo 5 | tel. 09 57 47 74 15)*

WHERE TO GO

ETNA ★ (143 D1) *(ﾉ K4)*

Europe's tallest active volcano is 33 km (20½ miles) from Catania. Mount Etna (3340 m/10,958 ft) can even be seen from the west coast of Sicily and Calabria on a clear day. Seen from the side facing inland, it is a yellowy, scorched, bald giant. It only turns a light green in spring when the grass grows. Its snowy cap doesn't always melt completely even in summer.

The best places from which to start exploring Etna's south side are *Nicolosi, Trecastagni* and *Zafferana Etnea*, from which it

is only approx. 20 km (12½ miles) *Rifugio Sapienza (1881 m/6170 ft)*, where the tarmac road ends and the AST buses from Catania and Nicolosi stop *(depart from Catania/station square daily 8.15am, in summer also Mon–Sat 11.20 am, Nicolosi daily 9am/12.30pm, return from Rifugio daily 4.30pm, in summer also Mon–Sat 10.45am; travel time 2 hours). Rifugio Sapienza (24 rooms | tel. 0 95 91 53 21 | www.rifugiosapienza.com | Budget)* has been extended and turned into a simple hotel. 500 m further on is the more comfortable hotel *Corsaro (20 rooms | tel. 09 59 14 22 | www.hotelco rsaro.it | Moderate)*. This is where the ● *cable car (daily 9am–4.15 pm (last ascent), in the winter until 3.45pm | tel. 0 95 91 41 41 | www.funiviaetna.com)* leaves from, the top of which is at an altitude of 2500 m (8200 ft). Off-road minibuses can take you further up the track as far as *Torre del Filosofo (2919 m/9576 ft)*. A return journey with a guide costs around 65 euros.

Colourful, loud and fascinating: the fish market at Porta Uzeda sells more than just seafood

When Etna erupts, lava up to 1500°C pours down its flanks

Guides for the summit can be booked at the cable car base station. There is no way-marked route. Tours on one's own initiative are only allowed as far as Torre del Filosofo and can be dangerous, especially when there is volcanic activity or fog suddenly descends. The temperature of molten lava is 800–1500°C! (1500–2800° F) Volcanic bombs are projected at supersonic speeds and can weigh up to more than 1 tonne. Close-up photos are best taken using a telephoto lens. The cordoned off areas are to keep visitors out of danger.

The eruptions in December 2015 were the most severe for decades. In March 2017, air traffic had to be interrupted because of ash particles in the air.

Piano Provenzana and *Rifugio Sapienza* are the principal starting points for tours up to the top of the volcano. Information from the *Mountain Guides' Office* in Nicolosi *(tel. 09 57 97 14 55 | www.etnaguide.eu)* or in Linguaglossa *(tel. 09 57 77 45 02 | www. guidetnanord.com)*. Up-to-date information about the Etna region can be found online, for example under: *www.ct.ingv.it*, *www.etnaexperience.com* and *www.etna*

trekking.com. Choose from one of the mountain tours organised by geologists Marco and Fabrizio. English-speaking tours available: *Etna Moving (Via G. Mameli 54 | Mascalucia | mobile tel. 37 79 80 41 42 | www.etnamoving.com)*. Winter clothing and hiking boots are essential. And start out early – the summit is often in the clouds later in the day. The hiking season is from mid May until the end of October. You will pass recent lava fields that smothered woods, fields and gardens on your way to the summit. After just a few years the surface of lava turns from a dark black to a matte grey and the first pioneer plants start to take hold. After 20 years, gorse spreads rapidly. In the early summer the sea of yellow is the most dominant colour on the slopes of the volcano. Forests, mostly of mountain pine and sweet chestnut, prevail. Above 1800 m (5900 ft), only low-growing shrubs and herbal plants can survive in this volcanic desert.

Nicolosi is the starting point for excursions from the south. Just above it there are waymarked walks to the *Pineta Monti Rossi* (the crater created in 1669). Information on the state of roads, the cable car, shelters and guided hikes: *Servizio Turistico Regionale (Via Martiri d'Ungheria 36–38 | tel. 0 95 91 15 05)*. Offices of the Etna Nature Park: *Via del Convento 45 | tel. 0 95 82 11 11 | www.parcoetna.it*

FERROVIA CIRCUMETNEA ★

A train ride around Sicily's mighty "ruler": the narrow gauge railway rattles and shakes its way around lots of bends on its way through this barren landscape on the west flank of Mount Etna. Having reached the highest point, *Maletto* (141 C6) *(🕮 K4)*, it carries on past *Randazzo* (140 C5) *(🕮 K4)* through a black lava desert from previous eruptions before dropping down to the coast through a fertile area of gardens and vineyards. The journey (never on Sundays) from *Catania Borgo* to *Randazzo* takes 2 hours; it is another 75 minutes from there to *Giarre* (143 E1) *(🕮 K5)*, from where there are connections to Catania and Messina. It is worth skipping a train in Randazzo and taking a walk through the Old Town which is built entirely of black volcanic rock and visiting the Norman cathedral. Gourmets should not miss a visit to *Macelleria Spartá (Via Umberto 89)* where Nunzio sells Bronte pistachios, sheep's milk cheese marinated in fig juice and salami from the black Nebrodi pig. Information under *www.circumetnea.it*. Alternatively enjoy this photographic tour: *www.swisseduc.ch/stromboli/etna*

LINGUA-GLOSSA

(141 D6) *(🕮 K4)* This village (pop. 5400) lies amidst luxuriant vineyards and hazelnut groves on a lava flow.

As in other villages around Etna, Baroque architecture dominates. The main church possesses a valuable altar made of cherry wood. This is where the panoramic *Mareneve* route begins that links the north side of the volcano with the south.

SIGHTSEEING

There is a small museum on the local natural history and volcanology of Etna in the tourist information *Pro Loco* (see p. 40). *Open mornings | free admission*

SPORTS & ACTIVITIES

Piano Provenzana (140 C6) *(🕮 K4)* at an altitude of 1810 m (5938 ft) is the most important winter sports arena on Mount Etna and the starting point for 4 × 4 tours by *Etna Discovery (tel. 09 57 80 75 64 | www.etnadiscovery.it)* towards the summit. This is where the 20 km (12½ miles) *Mareneve* route ("sea and snow") ends.

Up the side of the volcano: hiking up to the craters on Etna's summit

In autumn 2002, this plateau with its hotels, cabins, cable car and forests was buried under molten lava. The congealed black flows are more than impressive. Only the very experienced should attempt a hike to the summit on foot or by mountainbike after having contacted local guides beforehand.

WHERE TO STAY

AGRITURISMO L'ANTICA VIGNA 🌑
Organic winery with simple, well-maintained rooms, pool and homemade *maccheroni*. *10 rooms | on the Randazzo road in Montelaguardia | tel. 34 94 02 29 02 | www.anticavigna.it | Budget*

LOW BUDGET

🌊 *Ostello Odyssey (Via Paternò di Biscari 13 | tel. 0 94 22 45 33 | www.taorminaodyssey.com):* youth hostel with 2 and 4 bed dorms in a modern part of Taormina.

The, family-run hotel *California (Via del Sole 9 | tel. 0 35 12 03 49 75 | www.hotelcaliforniamilazzo.it)* right in the middle of the Old Town in Milazzo has 12 quiet rooms.

The youth hostel *Ostello Agorà (62 beds | Piazza Currò 6 | tel. 09 57 23 30 10 | www.agorahostel.com),* in a grand old house, has its own trattoria.

Taormina's snack bar: baked cheese, aubergine fritters and many pizzas. *Antipasteria Varo (daily | Via Jean D'Orville 1b | tel. 09 42 62 80 49 | www.pizzeriavaro.it)*

ZASH 🌊
Exclusive country hotel full of contrasts from its glass cube set against an ox-blood villa to lava walls combined with its ultra-smooth concrete pool. Pick your own blood oranges straight from the trees and sip a glass of the hotel's Nero d'Avola in front of an amazing panoramic setting with the coastline in the distance. Wine, art & architecture harmonize perfectly at this Etna hideaway. If you're lucky, you'll get room 3 with its sea-view patio. *10 rooms | Archi di Riposto | Strada Provinciale 2/I-II n. 60 | tel. 09 57 82 89 32 | www.zash.it | Expensive*

INFORMATION

Pro Loco (Piazza Annunziata 5 | tel. 0 95 64 30 94)

MESSINA

(141 E4) (*𝄞 L3*) For tourists coming by car or train from Calabria, Messina (pop. 237,000) is the gateway to the island. The city is modern with broad and straight roads.
And its brimming with life – especially in the principle shopping areas *Via San Martino*, the tree-lined *Piazza Cairoli* and *Via Garibaldi*. The heart of Messina can be found a little behind these around the *Piazza Duomo* with its magnificent cathedral. But even here as elsewhere in Messina, there are few stones that have been standing longer than 1908 when a terrible earthquake destroyed towns both sides of the straits, the *Stretto di Messina*.

SIGHTSEEING

CATHEDRAL
Originally built in 1197 in the Norman style and rebuilt after the earthquake in

1908 and again after bombing during the war in 1943. The belfry contains an astronomical clock from Strasbourg (1933) that includes a parade of figures with the city herooines Dina and Clarenza at noon.

MUSEO REGIONALE

The museum contains a picture gallery as well as displays of archeological finds, small artefacts and majolica. The most valuable exponents include an altarpiece by the Sicilian Antonello Da Messina and two paintings by Caravaggio, who lived on Sicily in 1608/09. *Tue–Sat 9am–7pm, Sun 9am–1pm | on the Punta del Faro road | admission 8 euros*

FOOD & DRINK

AL PADRINO

Lively trattoria in the centre with tasty plain food: lots of vegetables, pasta and fish. *Closed Sat evenings, Sun | Via Santa Cecilia 54 | tel. 09 02 92 10 00 | Budget*

INSIDER TIP LA DURLINDANA

The courtyard of this excellent restaurant is a popular retreat for locals to enjoy pumpkin squash flowers or salted cod *alla ghiotta:* in a caper and cherry tomato sauce. *Daily | Via Nicola Fabrizi 143–145 | tel. 09 06 413156 | www.la durlindana.com | Moderate–Expensive*

WHERE TO STAY

LE CASE PINTE

B & B at the ferry port (Caronte) with a view of the straits. *3 rooms | Viale della Libertà 251 | tel. 0 90 36 24 09 | www. lecasepinte.com | Budget*

SCILLA E CARIDDI

This modern villa is surrounded by a large garden and furnished in the late 19th-

Messina Cathedral: simply magnificent from all angles

century European style. Good view of the *Stretto,* rooms named after Homer's *Odyssey. 8 rooms | Viale Annunziata | 3 km/2 miles northeast) | tel. 0 90 35 78 49 | www.scillaecariddi.com | Budget–Moderate*

INFORMATION

Servizio Turistico Regionale (Via dei Mille is.87/A n.270 | tel. 09 02 93 52 92)

WHERE TO GO

Ferries *(www.carontetourist.it)* leave every 40 minutes for the mainland at *Reggio di Calabria* (141 F4) (*M3*) where the *Museo Archeologico Nazionale (Tue–Sun 9am–8pm | Piazza Giuseppe*

De Nava 26 | admission 8 euros, Wed 6 euros) exhibits the extremely well preserved Greek bronzes of naked bearded warriors, the *Bronzi di Riace* (cast in the 5th century BC).

MILAZZO

(141 D4) *(Ⓜ L3)* **The town (pop. 31,000) is at the beginning of a small peninsula which has several good beaches below the cliffs around Capo Milazzo.**
The pretty *Old Town* with its Spanish castle, Baroque cathedral and San Francesco di Paolo monastery, located above the ferry port for crossings to the Aeolian Islands and Naples, is surrounded by a massive circle wall. Information: *AAST (Piazza Duilio 20 | tel. 09 09 22 28 65)*

FOOD & DRINK

L'UGGHIULARU
Giuseppe Cannistra serves sword fish rolls, deep-fried red mullet, black squid spaghetti and pistachio truffle ice cream in the delightful courtyard. *Closed Wed | Via Tonnara 36 | tel. 09 09 28 43 84 | www.osterialugghiularu.it | Moderate*

WHERE TO STAY

PETIT HOTEL ⚓ 🌸
Restored to exacting environmental standards, restaurant with organic "Libera Terra" products. *9 rooms | Via dei Mille 37 | tel. 09 09 28 67 84 | www.petithotel.it | Budget–Moderate*

WHERE TO GO

SAN FRATELLO AND THE NEBRODI MOUNTAINS (140 B5) *(Ⓜ J3–4)*
In Sant'Agata di Militello, the road over the pass forks off to *Cesarò* and leads into

the heart of the *Nebrodi Park (www.parcodeinebrodi.it)* some 100 km (62 miles) further on. Its 1800 m (5900 ft) high mountain range is covered in extensive grazing land and thick beech woods. *San Fratello* is a typical mountain village well known for horse breeding.

TINDARI ★ ⚓ (140 C4) *(Ⓜ K3)*
The cliff of Tindari, 30 km (18½ miles) west of Milazzo, is a landmark on the north coast that cannot be missed. Below the 260 m (850 ft) high cliff face of the promontory, a sandbank enclosing a seawater lagoon and lakes stretches into the bay. The Black Madonna in the *pilgrimage church* attracts the faithful from all of Sicily. The sandbank and the Aeolian Islands can be seen from the square in front of the church. The plateau is the site of the *ancient city of Tyndaris (daily 9am–1 hr before sunset | admission 6 euros)* with an amphitheatre, basilica and the ruins of a city wall. The organic 🌸 *Agriturismo Santa Margh-*

erita estate *(18 rooms, 2 flats | tel. 0 94 13 97 03 | www.agriturismosantamarg herita.com | Budget–Moderate)* has a garden overlooking the sea, a restaurant, riding stables and mountainbikes for hire.

TAORMINA

MAP INSIDE BACK COVER
(141 D6) *(ΩΩ L4)* **The best known and most-visited holiday destination on Sicily, ☼ Taormina (pop. 11,000), is situated on a prominent hill at the end of the Peloritani mountain ridge high above the sea with an unforgettable view of Etna.**

The town centre is surrounded by villas and hotels dating from the 19th and 20th centuries. The picture of an enchanting medieval town unfurls to either side of the main shop-lined street, the *Corso Umberto*, between the town gates *Porta Messina* and *Porta Catania*, with castel-lated palaces, alleyways and small squares all linked by steps. The outskirts of Taormina suffer from the traffic; the centre is however an oasis. The *Piazza IX Aprile* half-way down the Corso, with its gate into the heart of the Old Town is a meeting place at all times of day, and the famous *Caffè Wunderbar* with the best view of Etna and the coast.

SIGHTSEEING

CATHEDRAL

The cathedral with its castellated façade dates from Norman times. The interior is plain. The *Baroque fountain with the Centaur*, Taormina's emblem, graces the square outside.

PALAZZO CORVAIA

The *palazzo* is one of the elegant palaces of the nobility dating from Norman times. The interior houses a folk museum (irregular opening times) and the tourist information office.

The view from the Teatro Greco-Romano over Taormina and the coastline extends for miles

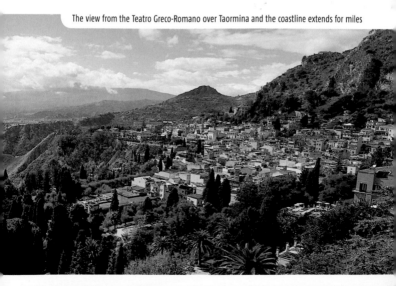

TEATRO GRECO-ROMANO ⭐ 🌿

The most impressive view of the coastline and the huge volcano can be enjoyed from the semicircle of this amphitheatre. It was hewn out of the stones in the 3rd century BC, in Hellenic times. In the 2nd century BC, the Romans converted it into an arena seating more than 5000 spectators. In the summer it serves as a backdrop for modern theatre and music performances. *May–Aug daily 9am–7pm, otherwise until approx. 1 hr before sunset | admission 10 euros*

FOOD & DRINK

AL GIARDINO

Daniele Puglia and his mother run one of the last surviving family trattorias in Taormina near the city park. *Closed Mon (open daily in summer) | Via Bagnoli Croci 84 | mobile tel. 33 93 00 17 20 | www.algiardinonet | Budget*

SHOPPING

KERAMEION

Not the usual touristy ceramics sold here. Authentic art impressions of swarms of sword fish, orange gardens and Mount Etna. This shop specialises in glazed mini tiles, a perfect souvenir. *Corso Umberto 198 | www.kerameion.com*

PASTICCERIA D'AMORE

A sweetly smelling confectionery which conjures up sugary delights such as orange and pistachio marzipan in its tiny *laboratorio.* Pastries are served in pretty marionette boxes. *Via Costantino Patricio 28 | www.pasticceriadamore.it*

BEACHES

The *Isola Bella* and *Mazzarò* beaches have large pebbles and are very crowded.

There's more room in *Letoianni* to the north, and *Capo Schisò* and *San Marco* to the south. The quickest way to get to Mazzarò is by cable car. Buses to the beaches run frequently between Capo Schisò and Letoianni.

ENTERTAINMENT

The *Corso Umberto* and the *piazza* next to the clocktower are the liveliest places. Discos are generally more on the outskirts.

BAR DELL' HOTEL METROPOLE 🌿

Sip champagne on the hotel's splendid terrace with sea view. *Corso Umberto 154 | near the Piazza*

WHERE TO STAY

GRAND HOTEL TIMEO & VILLA FLORA

This elegant villa set in lovely gardens was the first hotel in Taormina. *73 rooms | Via Teatro Greco 59 | tel. 0 94 26 27 02 00 | www.grandhoteltimeo.com | Expensive*

ISOCO GUEST HOUSE

Garden and five individually furnished rooms, some with a sea view. Owner Michele Scimone warmly welcomes all his guests. Book early! *Via Salita Branco 2 | tel. 0 94 22 36 79 | www.isoco.it | Budget*

INSIDER TIP ▶ VILLA SCHULER 🌿

Villa with individually served breakfast in the garden and a lovely view of the coast. *26 rooms | Piazzetta Bastione 16 | tel. 0 94 22 34 81 | www.hotelvillaschuler.com | Moderate–Expensive*

INFORMATION

Servizio Turistico Regionale (Palazzo Corvaja | tel. 0 94 22 32 43)

WHERE TO GO

ALCANTARA GORGE ★ (141 D5) (*K4*)
18 km (11 miles) west of Taormina the River Alcantara and its waterfalls have cut a narrow gorge through the basalt up to 50 m (165 ft) deep. Can be accessed down steps from the road to *Francavilla* as well as by a lift *(7–13 euros, depending on the season)*. Have fun bathing in the nearby *Spray Park (www.golealcantara.it)*. Or climb barefoot through the cold water while bodyrafting (you can hire wellies and neopren suits). You can also hike one of the signposted nature trails *(www.parcoalcantara.it)*. Enjoy local lamb dishes at the *Trattoria Rapisardi (daily | Via Roma 63 | Francavilla | tel. 09 42 98 13 41 | Budget)*.

CASTELMOLA (141 D5) (*L4*)
This tiny mountain eyrie with its Etna views (ruins of the *castello*) is 5 km (3 miles) away, almost vertically above Taormina, reachable by bus. Slightly further down is the hotel *Villa Sonia (44 rooms | tel. 0 94 22 80 82 | www.hotelvillasonia.com | Moderate–Expensive)*.

GIARDINI-NAXOS (141 D6) (*L4*)
This tourist resort famous for its beaches is 6 km (3¾ miles) south of Taormina, wedged in between main roads and the railway line. The shore area is however particularly attractive near the *excavation site of Ancient Naxos*, the oldest Greek city on Sicily with impressive megalithic stone walls. The resort hotel *Arathena Rocks (49 rooms | tel. 0 94 25 13 49 | www.chincherinihotels.com | Moderate)* is right on the sea in a private park.

SAVOCA (141 D–E5) (*L4*)
Mummified corpses can be seen in the *Chiesa dei Cappuccini* in this mountain village 24 km (15 miles) to the north in the Peloritani Mountains. The Norman and Byzantine church INSIDER TIP *Pietro e Paolo*, which boasts Arabian intarsia work and steep-sided domes, is situated below Siculo near Scifi in the *Fiumara d'Agrò* valley in a lemon grove.

Water broke the basalt in the Alcantara Gorge

THE SOUTHEAST

Sicilians often talk about the "island on the island". Rising behind the flat coastal plains with their dense plantations of almond trees, olive groves and citrus fruit, is the karst landscape of gorges and rivers of the Monti Iblei mountains, which rise to almost 600 m (1968 ft).

The lush fertile plains are in stark contrast to the sparse vegetation in the mountains where treeless grazing land, divided by miles of stone walls and with a scattering of isolated farms, stretches as far as the horizon. Trees grow in profusion in the valleys following the course of the streams and rivers, and gorges boast dense jungles of oleander, tree-high Spanish cane, violet blossoming Monk's Pepper and brambles. The upper flanks of the gorges that can be reached from the plains above, were the first places to be settled. Since 2007, the large limestone plateau with its deep ravines has been waiting to become Sicily's first national park.

Ispica, Modica and the twin towns of Ragusa and Ibla have spectacular locations, as does the isolated necropolis of Pantalica. All have been built in the light-coloured limestone of the area which is easy to work when first quarried before becoming harder after contact with the air and taking on a grey or dark yellow patina. No other stone enabled sculptors to live out their fantasies so easily. Portals with faces and ornamental scrolling, sills and balconies, façades with gnomes, nymphs,

Photo: Noto, San Nicolo (left) and San Salvatore (centre)

Contrasting Sicilian highlights: fertile plains, barren mountains, and cities from the ancient to the Baroque

monsters, squiggles and pillars are characteristic features of these towns. This is especially true of those rebuilt after the devastating earthquake of 1693.

CALTAGIRONE

(142 B3) (*H–J6*) ⭐ **Caltagirone (pop. 38,000) with its church towers and domes can be seen from a long way away on a mountain peak.**

The streets are narrow and, apart from the famous *majolica staircase*, there are many other plain flights of steps. The *grand staircase* of 1608, with its decorative ceramic tiles of a more recent date, connects the lower town with the *Palazzo della Corte Capitaniale* and the main square with the principle church, *Santa Maria al Monte*, in the upper town. In the *Villa Comunale* in the park next to the ceramics museum is the *Teatrino*, a pavilion decorated with majolica tiles.

142 steps with colourful Majolica tiles lead to Caltagirone's upper town and Santa Maria al Monte

SIGHTSEEING

MUSEO DELLA CERAMICA ●

Ceramics from Antiquity to the present day and Sicilian majolica from the Renaissance and Baroque periods. *Mon–Sat 9am–6.30pm, Sun 10am–6.30pm | Giardino Pubblico | admission 4 euros*

FOOD & DRINK

CORIA

Two small dining rooms near the Staircase and two chefs who like experimenting and who love fresh herbs and seafood. Try the couscous with fish sauce, the sweet and sour stuffed rabbit or the orange salad. *Closed Sun and Mon lunchtime | Via Infermeria 24 | tel. 09 32 65 96 | www.ristorantecoria.it | Moderate*

POMARA

Rustic restaurant in neighbouring *San Michele di Ganzaria*, aromatic country cooking with big meat portions. Hotel *(40 rooms). tel. 09 33 97 69 76 | www. hotelpomara.com | Moderate*

SHOPPING

CERAMICS

Many quality pieces are still made traditionally in the ceramic workshops in Caltagirone, where the decoration and glazing of expensive items is carried out with meticulous precision. If you like, you can also watch the craftsmen at work in their studios in the Old Town. Works are exhibited in the courtyard of the *Palazzo Corte Capitaniale* and in the shops in the *Galleria Sturzo.*

WHERE TO STAY

IL PICCOLO ATTICO

B & B in the middle of the Old Town not far from the Staircase, lovely ☀ roof terrace with a view over the town. *3 rooms, 1 flat | Via Infermeria 82 | tel. 0 93 32 15 88 | www.ilpiccoloattico.it | Budget*

INFORMATION

Ufficio turistico unificato (Via Duomo 15 | tel. 09 33 49 08 36 | www.comune. caltagirone.ct.it)

ENNA

(142 A2) *(⚏ H5)* **The provincial capital** ☼ **Enna (pop. 28,000) at more than 900 m/2953 ft, is called the "belvedere of Sicily" due to its views over central Sicily and the mountain village Calascibetta opposite, Mount Etna and the mountains to the north.**

The fortifications from the Norman era and the Hohenstaufen dynasty, such as the *Castello di Lombardia* with the *Torre Pisana* at the highest point of the town, as well as the octagonal tower, the *Torre di Federico II*, allegedly designed by Emperor Frederick II, are well worth seeing.

FOOD & DRINK

LA RUSTICA
Popular trattoria for business lunches: pasta with cauliflower, lentil soup and lamb offal. *Closed Sun | Via Gagliano Castelferrato | tel. 0 93 52 55 22 | Budget*

ENTERTAINMENT

AL KENISA
If the Pope knew! An old secular Baroque Church is now home to a *caffè letterario,* a literature coffee shop. Concerts in the evenings, cocktail and wine bar. *Tue–Sun 3pm–1am | Via Roma 481 | tel. 09 35 50 09 72 | alkenisa.blogspot.com*

WHERE TO STAY

LA CASA DEL POETA
B & B in a 19th-century country house above Lago Pergusa, surrounded by cypress and olive trees. Modern interior, decorated with literary texts and graphic works; reading room, pool. ✿ Organic breakfast. *26 rooms | mobile tel. 32 96 27 49 18 | www.lacasadelpoeta.it | Moderate*

INFORMATION

At *Servizio Turistico Regionale (Piazza Napoleone Colajanni 6 | tel. 09 35 50 08 75),* you get excellent, varied material on the region.

WHERE TO GO

MORGANTINA ☼ **(142 B2)** *(⚏ H6)*
The ancient city is 42 km (26 miles) southeast of Enna on a mountain ridge with views of the Etna and the sea. The wind and the silence dominate the 2000-year-old paved streets, the well-preserved amphitheatre and the huge terraced

MARCO POLO HIGHLIGHTS

★ **Caltagirone**
Flights of steps, palaces and churches are decorated with majolica tiles → **p. 47**

★ **Piazza Armerina**
Mosaics cover 3500 m²/37,674 sq ft in the Roman Villa del Casale → **p. 50**

★ **Noto**
This small Baroque town was planned on a grid system → **p. 51**

★ **Museo Archeologico**
A tour through the 15,000-year history of Syracuse → **p. 57**

★ **Ortygia**
Antiquity, the Middle Ages and the Baroque at close quarters → **p. 57**

★ **Pantalica**
More than 5000 tombs hewn into the rock → **p. 59**

agorà (daily 11am–7pm | admission 6 euros). INSIDERTIP Statues of gods from illicit excavations, previously at the Getty Museum in Los Angeles and since returned to Italy, are on show in *Aidone* in the *Museo Archeologico (daily 9am–7pm | admission 6 euros).*

PIAZZA ARMERINA ★ (142 A3) (⌘ H6)

This town with its colourful and silver church domes lies on a mountain ridge surrounded by eucalyptus groves, hazel woods and orchards, 34 km (21 miles) southeast of Enna. 5 km (3 miles) down a river valley, a turning leads to the excavation site of the ● *Villa Romana del Casale (April–Oct daily 9am–7pm (July/Aug Fri–Sun until 11pm), Nov–March 9am–5pm (last admission always 1 hr before) | admission 10 euros | www.villaromanadelcasale.it).* The floor mosaics from Antiquity of this World Heritage Site are among the most extensive and beautiful to have survived. The techniques and motifs suggest artists from North Africa. The villa was probably the hunting lodge of a Roman animal trader from the 4th century. The ground plan, under protective Plexiglass structures, is clearly recognisable: public and private quarters, thermal baths, halls, bed-chambers, privy, kitchen, servants' rooms and, at the centre, the peristyle, the internal garden surrounded by a colonnade. Raised walkways lead to the "Chamber of the Maidens" with its famous mosaic of girls performing sports in bikini-like garments.

The ☻ *Agriturismo Bannata (SS 117, km 41 | tel. 09 35 68 13 55 | www.agriturismobannata.it | Moderate, restaurant for house guests Budget)* is on the edge of a wood 6 km (3¾ miles) north of Piazza. Art exhibitions and music events are held in the rooms with natural stone and terracotta floors, modern furniture and antiques. Light food made to old recipes is served in the restaurant. Bread, biscuits, vegetables and wine come from their own organic production. *Al Fogher (closed Mon | tel. 09 35 68 41 23 | alfogher.sicilia.restaurant | Expensive)*, which serves excellent, imaginative Sicilian food, is located on the road to Enna after the turn to Morgantina (2 km/1¼ mile). Information: *Servizio Turistico Regionale (Via Generale Muscarà 15 | in the village, not at the villa! | tel. 09 35 68 02 01)*

SICILIA FASHION VILLAGE (142 B2) (⌘ J5)

30 km (18½ miles) east of Enna, right next to the motorway, is Sicily's largest outlet centre with 120 clothes shops, bars and restaurants, all built to look like a small 18th-century Sicilian town. *(Mon–Fri 10am–8pm, Sat/Sun 10am–9pm | A 19 Catania–Palermo, exit Dittaino | www.siciliaoutletvillage.it).*

LOW BUDGET

Good cheap food can be found in *Osteria Mariano (closed Tue | Vicolo Zuccalà 9 | tel. 0 93 16 74 44)* near the Fountain of Arethusa in Syracuse.

The youth hostel *Ostello il Castello (68 beds | Via Fratelli Bandiera 1 | mobile tel. 32 08 38 88 69 | www.ostellodinoto.it)* is in the castle in the Old Town of Noto.

The village trattoria *Osteria Locale (closed Tue | Via Dusmet 14 | tel. 09 31 87 39 23)* in Bucheri serves good-value meat and sheeps cheese, mushrooms and homemade pasta.

In *Raddusa*, 15 km (9 miles) further south, ●  *Casa-Museo del Tè (ViaGaribaldi 45 | free admission | advance booking necessary, tel. 0 95 66 21 93 | www.lacasa delte.it | Budget)* traces the history of tea with 600 different sorts and 500 teapots from all over the world. You can take part in a tea ceremony in the *salon* or enjoy the Asian-style food and thereby support projects in the third world.

NOTO

(143 D5) (⚏ K7) The Baroque town of ★ Noto (pop. 24,000) is a Unesco World Heritage Site at the foot of the Hyblaean Mountains above the coastal plain with dense olive groves as shady as a woods. The medieval *Noto Antica* fell victim to the earthquake of 1693. The ruins can be seen 9 km (5.6 miles) further inland.

SIGHTSEEING

THE TOWN OF PALACES

The main churches, palaces, squares and flights of steps can be found in the elegant district of Noto along the three parallel main thoroughfares. The central one, the *Corso Vittorio Emanuele*, finishes at the representative town gates. It covers a large area with parks and squares and is lined by town palaces, opening up half-way down to the *Piazza Duomo* with a broad view of steps and façades. This is where the spiritual and worldly centres of power stand face to face – the *cathedral* and the *Palazzo Ducezio*.

FOOD & DRINK

CROCIFISSO ⚏

TV chef Marco Baglieri promotes "zero km" cooking: all ingredients come from

Pure Baroque: the balcony supports at the Palazzo Villadorato in Noto

the nearest sources. *Closed Wed | Via Principe Umberto 46 | tel. 09 31 57 11 51 | www.ristorantecrocifisso.it | Budget*

BEACHES & SPORTS

Swimming and bird-watching are two options on the fine sandy beach in *Marina di Noto*, hiking and swimming in the *Vendicari* nature reserve, and swimming in the clean waters of the *Cava Grande (Noto–Palazzolo road)*.

WHERE TO STAY

TERRA DI SOLIMANO ⊗
(143 D5) (🗺 K7)

This organically-run historical manor on the road to Noto Antica offers bed and breakfast. *8 rooms | tel. 09 31 83 66 06 | www.terradisolimano.it | Budget*

VILLA CANISELLO

Former farmhouse on the edge of the Old Town with a large garden. *6 rooms | Via Pavese 1 | tel. 09 31 83 57 93 | www.villa canisello.it | Budget*

WHERE TO GO

CAVA D'ISPICA (142 C5) (🗺 J–K8)

The 14 km (8.7 miles) long karst gorge ends just below the Baroque town of *Ispica*, 27 km (17 miles) southwest of Noto. The main access to the gorge, which boasts Byzantine rock churches and subterranean catacombs *(May–Oct daily 9am–6.30pm | 4 euros)* is on the road from Rosolini to Modica. The *Parco della Forza (May–Oct daily 9am–6.30pm | 2 euros)* in Ispica, with its cave churches and wall fragments, takes you an easy 3 km (1¾ mile) into the gorge. Locals swear by the shrimp carpaccio prepared by *Donna Patrizia (daily | Via Platamone 26 | mobile tel. 34 95 14 10 74 | Moderate–Expensive)* in nearby Rosolini.

NOTO ANTICA & PALAZZOLO ACREIDE

While on this 96 km (60 miles) tour, take the road in Noto to the *Convento della Scala*, an isolated Baroque pilgrimage church. Just a little further on, park the car on the approach road to *Noto Antica* (143 D5) (🗺 K7). The massive gateway and walls are the most impressive remains of this town destroyed in 1693, located on a high plain. Here and there traces of walls can be seen above the weeds, including columns and church portals on the near end of the plateau.

Cava Grande: the little River Cassíbile carved out these wonderful "bathtubs"

Returning to the main road, the 287, you can make a 6 km (3¾ miles) detour along the by-road to Avola to INSIDER TIP *Cava Grande*, a broad gorge approached down a steep, rocky path from the car park. Further paths lead along the crystal-clear river with waterfalls, lakes and sandbanks. Good shoes are needed to climb down into the gorge 250 m/820 ft below, as the path can be slippery.

Palazzolo Acreide (143 D4) (*∅ K7*) dominates a hill, the highest point of which was the site occupied by the ancient town Akrai. Baroque craftsmen have created an abundance of decorative elements, including faces and mythological figures, out of soft yellow limestone and wrought iron. The façades around the huge piazza are especially richly decorated. From here, a passage leads to the folk museum, *Casa Museo Antonino Uccello (Mon–Sat 9am–7pm, 1st/3rd Sun 9am–71.30 pm, 2nd/4th Sun 2pm–7.30pm | admission 2 euros)*. Regional food is served in *Trattoria Andrea (closed Tue | Via G. Judica 4 | tel. 09 31 88 14 88 | Budget)*. Enjoy far-reaching views over the southeast of Sicily from the ancient ✲ *Acropolis (daily 8am–6.30pm | admission 4 euros)* which has a small amphitheatre.

PORTO PALO DI CAPO PASSERO (143 E6) (*∅ K8*)

This small town, 28 km (17½ miles) from Noto on Sicily's southernmost point, with its busy fishing port, has become a popular holiday destination thanks to the extensive dunes and beaches to the north near *Vendicari* and the sandy bays. Windsurfers come for the strong winds. Plain accommodation and good food is available in the modern holiday hotels *Jonic (12 rooms | tel. 09 31 84 27 23 | www. hoteljonic.eu | Budget)* and *Vittorio (25 rooms | tel. 09 31 84 21 81 | www.ris torantevittorio.it | Budget–Moderate)*.

The terrace of the picturesque celebhangout *Cialoma (Piazza Regina Margherita 23 | tel. 09 31 84 17 72 | Moderate)* in *Marzamemi*, the neighbouring fishing village that consists of a few flat-roofed stone huts, often serves as a location for Italian TV crews.

INSIDER TIP VENDICARI & VILLA ROMANA TELLARO (143 D6) (*∅ K8*)

Vendicari Nature Reserve (www.riserva-vendicari.it) incorporates wide sandy beaches, dunes with Mediterranean *macchia*, swamps and lagoons, which are a unique paradise for birds, is 8 km (5 miles) long and up to 1.5 km/1 mile wide. 250 different breeds of bird live here, including flamingos, storks, herons, ibis and spoonbills.

The *Villa Romana Tellaro (daily 9am–7pm | admission 6 euros)* is on the Porto Palo road right next to the sea, at the north boundary of Vendicari Nature Reserve. Late Roman mosaics of hunting scenes and heroic figures from the *Iliad* can now be viewed after 30 years of excavation.

RAGUSA

(142 C5) (*∅ J7*) **The Baroque jewel of Ragusa (pop. 74,000), fascinatingly towering above deep canyons, is the capital of the smallest and wealthiest province on Sicily. The oil fields, now fully exhausted, launched a short industrial boom around 1960.**

The novels in the "Commissario Montalbano" series were filmed for television in the little towns and coastal villages in this province. His house is in Puntasecca; Donnalucata is the port of the fictional town "Vigata". The Baroque setting of Ragusa Ibla, Scicli and Modica turned the series into a visual delight.

Towering over the streets around Ibla: the dome of the Duomo di San Giorgio

Ragusa has two centres: the more modern *Ragusa* with its wide streets, and the small Baroque *Ibla* of the nobility, clerics, craftspeople and agricultural workers, with its flights of steps, narrow alleyways and little squares.

SIGHTSEEING

DUOMO DI SAN GIORGIO

The main church in Ibla, with its imposing façade and flight of steps, is an exceptional example of Baroque style in Sicily.

SAN GIORGIO VECCHIO ☆

The ruins of a Norman church with a lovely portal. From the park behind you have a fantastic view of the town above and the gorge.

FOOD & DRINK

KONZA

A fashionable, rustic-style haunt of locals, serving authentic *pizzoli* (pizza rolls). Slow service. *Closed lunchtime | Via Mariannina Coffa 9 | tel. 09 32 68 65 61 | www.konza. it | Budget*

MAJORE

Restaurant in the centre of the neighbouring village Chiaramonte Gulfi. Popular for stuffed pork chops since 1896. *Closed Mon and in July | Via Martiri Ungheresi 12 | tel. 09 32 92 80 19 | www. majore.it | Budget*

INSIDER TIP ▶ PASTICCERIA DI PASQUALE

One of Italy's most tempting patisseries. *Torta Savoia,* marzipan and savoury filled arancini. Exclusive atmosphere. *Closed Mon | Corso Vittorio Veneto 104 | tel. 09 32 62 46 35 | www.pasticceriadi pasquale.com*

WHERE TO STAY

AGRITURISMO VILLA ZOTTOPERA ☺

17th-century manorial farm, excellent food, cookery courses, organic production of olive oil, wine and vegetables. *5 flats | 8 km (5 miles) towards Chiaramonte | tel. 09 32 24 40 18 | www. villazottopera.it | Moderate*

MONTREAL

Centrally located town hotel. *50 rooms | Via San Giuseppe 14 | tel. 09 32 62 11 33 | www.montrealhotel.it | Moderate*

INFORMATION

Infotourist (Piazza San Giovanni | tel. 09 32 68 47 80 | www.comune.ragusa.gov. it/turismo/infotourist.html)

WHERE TO GO

CASTELLO DI DONNAFUGATA
(142 B5) (*ØØ J7*)
Leopard dreams: This palace with park and labyrinth 15 km (9 miles) from Ragusa was redecorated in a Neo-Moorish style in the 19th century, the interior decked out with mirrors, frescos and antique furniture *(Tue, Thu, Sun 9am–1pm, 2.45pm–4.30/5.30pm, Wed, Fri, Sat 9am–1pm | admission incl. park 8 euros)*. Luchino Visconti was inspired for "The Leopard" here. The *Trattoria Al Castello (closed Mon | tel. 09 32 61 92 60 | www.alcastellodonnafugata.com | Budget)* which serves simple dishes is housed in the former stables.

MODICA (142 C5) (*ØØ J7*)
The former capital of the county of Modica, identical to the present-day province of Ragusa, is 15 km (9 miles) south at the base of two karst gorges that meet at the central square. The Old Town, with its narrow alleyways and flights of steps, climbs the steep slopes, whereas the two main streets with their prome-nades, churches and palaces of the nobil-ity run along the valley. The dominant architectural style here is also Baroque, fine examples of which are the main church, *San Pietro* in the lower town, and *San Giorgio* with five portals and a flight of 250 steps.
The B&B *Talía (6 rooms | Via Exaudinos 9 | tel. 09 32 75 20 75 | Expensive)* stands for *slow living* with an oriental touch. At *Monoresort (5 flats | tel. 09 32 45 33 08 | www.monoresort.com | Expensive)* you

stay in restored houses with modern designer interiors. In the elegant *Fattoria delle Torri (closed Sun evening and Mon | Vico Napolitano 14 | tel. 09 32 75 12 86 | Moderate)* in the middle of the Old Town, you can eat like in the olden days.
Modica is the earliest Sicilian centre of the chocolate industry. The *Corso Umberto* is perfect for a "chocolate tour": for example in *Antica Dolceria Bonajuto*, the *Laboratorio Dolciario Don Giuseppe Puglisi* or in ☺ *Quetzal*, a *bottega solidale*, in which fairtrade products are processed. *Information: Ufficio Turismo (Corso Umberto 141 | tel. 09 32 75 92 04)*
The neighbouring Baroque town *Scicli* (pop. 27,000), which is only a few roads wide, winds its way down a gorge. You can get a good impression of its unusual location from the church of San Matteo further up. Art historians consider the *Palazzo Beneventano* to be one of the most imaginative Baroque buildings on the island.

SYRACUSE

▓▓▓ **MAP ON P. 56**
▓▓▓ (143 E4) (*ØØ L7*) **Syracuse by day, Siracusa by night! In its heyday, this city was the creative mind of Ancient Greece**

🏙 **WHERE TO START?**
Ortygia: Syracuse's station is on the outskirts of the city but a good bus service operates to the Old Town of Ortygia on the island. Buses 1 and 2 connect the Old Town with the excavation sites, bus 3 with the museum, both in the modern city on the mainland. The Parcheggio Telete car park is in the north of the island.

SYRACUSE

and the birthplace of comedy, cooking, the ideal Platonism state and European Christianity.

The safe natural harbour and the fresh-water source of the nymph Arethusa in mythology attracted colonists from Corinth from an early date. With a reputed population of half a million, this Ancient city with its gigantic quarries was far bigger than its size today.

However today, the provincial capital of *Siracusa* (pop. 122,000) with its fascinating monuments is fully on a par with its ancient rival. Its historical centre with medieval lanes is situated on the "quail island" of *Ortygia;* a romantic district which has seen a recent revamp and now houses boutique hotels, restaurants with products from the Monti Iblei and local fashion labels. In the evenings, young couples dress

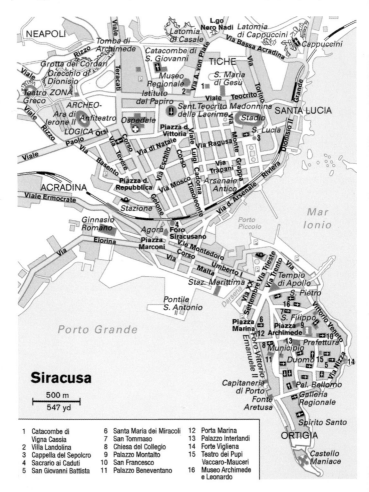

Siracusa

500 m
547 yd

Splendid buildings surround the cathedral square in Ortigia such as the Palazzo Beneventano del Bosco

to the nines to meet for a sundowner on the Baroque Cathedral Square or in one of the bars along the seafront at *Lungomare Alfeo.* Amphitheatre-style entertainment can still be found at the *Opera dei pupi* (see p. 119) when the marionettes are dancing or at the *Teatro Greco* (see p. 58) for performances of Ancient Greek tragedies.

SIGHTSEEING

GALLERIA REGIONALE IN THE PALAZZO BELLOMO

Most tourists come to this medieval palace in Ortygia to see the "Annunciation", a masterpiece by the Early Renaissance painter, Antonello da Messina. *Tue–Sat 9am–7pm, Sun 9am–1pm | Via Capodieci 16 | admission 8 euros*

MUSEO ARCHEOLOGICO ★

Sicily's largest museum contains prehistoric artefacts as well as finds from Ancient Greek and Roman sites. Highlights include the *Venus Landolina* and an archaic *kouros* – a statue of a male youth – made of limestone. *Tue–Sat 9am–6pm, Sun 9am–1pm | Viale Teocrito 66 | admission 8 euros*

MUSEO ARCHIMEDE E LEONARDO

Real-life wargames are on display at this museum showing how the mathematician Archimedes deployed cranes and concave mirrors in an attempt to defect the attacking Roman navy. However, all was in vain as Syracuse was conquered in 212 B.C. and Archimedes was killed by a marauding soldier. Since 2016, the warfare can be compared to the models of Leonardo da Vinci. *Daily 10.30am–8pm (winter until 7pm) | Via Vicenzo Mirabella 31 | admission 6.50 euros*

ORTYGIA ★

The bridge from the mainland leads to *Piazza Pancali*, where the gigantic dressed stones and columns of the *Temple of Apollo* (6th century BC) cannot be missed. In the morning, the square and the roads nearby leading to *Porto Piccolo* – the fishing port – is a sea of market stalls and people. *Corso Matteotti* leads to *Piazza Archimede*, into the heart of the Old Town. The majority of the palaces line the square and the promenade *Via Maestranza* that leads off it.

The magnificent *Piazza Duomo* is dominated by the cathedral's massive Baroque façade that is subdivided by columns. The *Temple of Athena (daily 10am–6.30pm | admission 2 euros)* from the 5th century BC, turned into a church, lies behind it. In the abbey church ● *Santa Lucia alla Badia (Tue–Sun 11am–4pm | free admission),* Caravaggio's masterpiece "Burial of St. Lucy"" from 1608 can be seen. The *Fountain of Arethusa* has its source below the promenade along the shore and gushes into a fishpond planted with papyrus. 〰 *Castello Maniace (Mon noon–3.45pm, Tue–Sun 8.30am–12.30pm | admission 4 euros),* the medieval fortress, is part of the former defensive wall and offers wonderful views down the coast.

PARCO ARCHEOLOGICO DELLA NEAPOLI

The archeological area on the outskirts of the new town covers a small part of ancient Syracuse and several *latomie* – quarries from Antiquity. A shady path from the entrance leads to the *Roman amphitheatre,* largely hewn directly out of the rock face. Large public sacrifices were celebrated on the *Altar of Hieron* (198 m/650 ft long, 23 m/75 ft wide, 3rd century BC). The *Greek theatre,* with tiers also cut out of the rock, could seat more than 15,000 spectators. It is still used for classical performances. *Latomia del Paradiso* is the largest quarry in the ancient urban settlement and now a cool and shady park. The Ear of Dionysius is an artificial cave – a subterranean quarry – 65 m/213 ft long and 23 m/75 ft high, which was reputedly used as a prison. The unusual acoustics that make even whispers clearly audible, was perfect for listening to suspects. *Mon–Sat 8.30am–6.30pm (winter until 4.30pm), Sun 8.30am–1.45pm | admission 10 euros*

Tragedies have been performed in this Greek theatre since 470 BC

SAN GIOVANNI CATACOMBS

The extensive Early Christian catacombs can be accessed through San Giovanni church in modern Syracuse. *Daily 9.30am–12.30pm and 2.30pm–5.30pm | admission 8 euros*

SANTUARIO DELLA MADONNINA DELLE LACRIME

The plaster statue of the Virgin Mary, which has cried tears and performed miracles since 1953, is kept in a building with a diameter of 90 m/295 ft and a 76 m/250 ft-high conical roof ("lemon squeezer") that dominates the city.

FOOD & DRINK

DON CAMILLO

A wide selection of delicious seafood dishes prepared to traditional recipes. On the main road in Ortygia. *Closed Sun | Via Maestranza 96 | tel. 0 93 16 71 33 | www. ristorantedoncamillosiracusa.it | Expensive*

LA GAZZA LADRA

This tiny osteria serves antipasti with vegetables fresh from the market and fish salads. *Closed Mon and for lunch. | Via Cavour 8 | mobile tel. 34 00 60 24 28 | www.lagazzaladrasiracusa.com | Budget*

BEACHES & SPORTS

Good sandy beaches can be found in *Fontane Bianche (143 E5) (Ø L7)*. Walkers will enjoy a hike through the *Anapo Valley* and in *Pantalica*.

WHERE TO STAY

GUTKOWSKI

Intimate boutique hotel in authentic Mediterranean style with a sun terrace and sea views located on Ortygia's seafront. *25 rooms | Lungomare Vittorini 26 | tel. 09 31 46 58 61 | www. guthotel.it | Moderate*

INSIDER TIP TERRAUZZA SUL MARE ◉

This country home, run by the ceramicist Renata Emmolo, is on the Maddalena peninsula next to the sea. Organic produce. *9 flats | Via Blanco 8 | loc. Terrauzza | tel. 09 31 71 43 62 | www.terramar.it | Budget–Moderate*

INFORMATION

Servizio Turistico Regionale (Via Maestranza 33 | tel. 09 31 46 42 55 | www. comune.siracusa.it)

WHERE TO GO

FIUME CIANE (143 E4) (Ø L7)

This river, just 5 km (3 miles) long, comes from two sources in the limestone hills and enters the sea near the former salt works in Syracuse. The sources and the upper reaches are the only places in Europe where papyrus sedge occurs naturally. A 3 km (1¾ mile) long footpath along the river bank starts at the source on the road from Syracuse to Canicattini. One-hour ● *motorboat trips (Vella family | mobile tel. 36 87 29 60 40)* start at Anapo bridge on the Noto road.

PANTALICA ★ (143 D4) (Ø K7)

Pantalica is 50 km (31 miles) from Syracuse via Ferla or 35 km (22 miles) via Sortino. A road runs from both villages to the Necropolis of Pantalica created by the Sicel people. More than 5000 burial chambers from the late Neolithic period and Bronze Age, dug into the rock, line the sides of the Anapo and neighbouring valleys. They were later used as a safe refuge during turbulent periods. Only one villa from the 11th century BC has been excavated in the adjoining settlement.

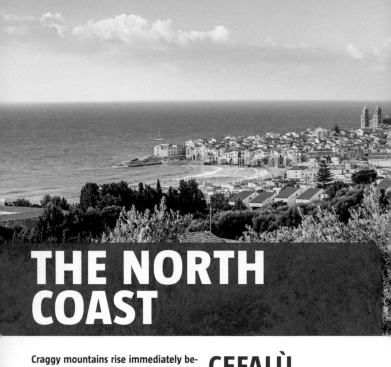

THE NORTH COAST

Craggy mountains rise immediately behind the northern coastline of Sicily. In
only a few places have rivers carved out
plains where the luxuriant orange plantations and orchards provide a stark contrast to the bare rock. The jagged plateaus of the foreland became the perfect
hideout of the Mafia.

The sea has formed wide bays enclosed
by promontories, such as the Gulf of
Castellammare, the large Gulf of Palermo
and the broad Gulf of Termini Imerese,
whose boundary is marked by the rock
above the cathedral city of Cefalù. This
adjoins the long stretch of coast until Capo
Orlando that lies at the foot of the
Madonie and Nebrodi mountains that
have since been made into regional
natural parks.

CEFALÙ

(139 D2) *(ᗰ G3)* **The massive Norman
cathedral of Cefalù (pop. 14,500) looks
like a toy set against the huge rocky
Rocca mountain.**

The roofs of the houses are clustered
around the landmark of this town that
was a burial place in the early Norman
period and had a brief heyday as an important harbour before falling into a deep
sleep like Sleeping Beauty until the 20th
century. This left the medieval town virtually unaltered. The *Corso Ruggero*, the
main street lined with austere palaces
with pointed arched windows, opens
onto the cathedral square. The Old Town
is protected from the sea by a huge wall

The lively, exhausting metropolis of Palermo, surrounded by nature reserves, dominates the north coast

whose lower part is made up of metre-high blocks from early history. To the west of the Old Town is a large bay followed by a promenade.

SIGHTSEEING

ARABIAN WASH HOUSE

In the middle of the narrow Old Town is a small square that leads to a row of stone basins under low arches where several springs emerge. The wash house dates from the Arabian era.

DUOMO DI CEFALÙ ★

The stones of this, the oldest Norman cathedral in Sicily (begun in 1131) and only completed after hundreds of years, speak volumes; the plain arches of the portico and the two massive, minaret-like towers are impressive. The archaic cloisters with the apse decorated with gold mosaics and the narrow transept all symbolise strength and power. *April–Oct daily 8.30am–6.30pm, Nov–March Mon–Sat 8.30am–1pm and 3.30pm–5pm, Sun 3.30pm–5pm*

MUSEO MANDRALISCA

Private collection of archeological finds and the famous portrait of an unknown man by Antonello da Messina. *Daily 9am–7pm (in August until 11pm) | Via Mandralisca 13 | admission 6 euros | www.fondazionemandralisca.it*

Fiumara d'Arte: an 18 m (59 ft) high sculpture in the Tusa valley

INSIDER TIP ▶ ROCCA DI CEFALÙ ☆

La Rocca towers 268 m/879 ft above the town, its vertical walls protecting it from being conquered. The only access is through a number of walls and gateways from Antiquity and the Middle Ages. Flights of steps and paths lead to cisterns, ruins of buildings and a pre-Roman temple in the Cyclopean style. Remember to take water with you and wear stout shoes. *Daily 9am–6pm | admission 4 euros*

FOOD & DRINK

CAFFÈ LETTERARIO LA GALLERIA

Right next to the cathedral. Cool bar and restaurant with snacks, newspapers, a gallery, Internet access and exhibitions.

Daily | Via Mandralisca 23 | tel. 09 21 42 02 11 | www.lagalleriacefalu.it | Budget

NASCA 2

Artichoke trattoria in the mountains of Cerda (139 D2) (*𝄞 F3*) with a variety of vegetable antipasti. Every year, the region (38 km/24 miles southwest of Cefalù) celebrates an artichoke festival, "Sagra del carciofo", and the famous vintage car race "Targa Florio". *Daily, lunchtime only | Strada statale 120/km 6.2 | mobile tel. 34 64 26 13 42 | www.trattorienascacerda.com | Moderate*

BEACHES & SPORTS

Beautiful natural beaches can be found in *Mazzaforno* (5 km/3 miles to the west), in *Capo Caldura* (2 km/1¼ miles to the east) and in *Capo Raisigerbi* near Finale di Pollina (139 E2) (*𝄞 G3*). You can hike 2 km (1¼ mile) in the direction of Gratteri to the *Fattoria Pianetti (tel. 09 21 42 18 90 | www.fattoriapianetti.com)*.

WHERE TO STAY

KALURA ☆

Sports hotel above the cliffs, 2 km (1¼ mile) east. Panoramic terrace, swimming platform, pebbly beach, mountainbiking, diving. *65 rooms | Caldura | tel. 09 21 42 13 54 | www.hotel-kalura.com | Moderate–Expensive*

INFORMATION

Servizio Turistico Regionale (Corso Ruggero 77 | tel. 09 21 42 10 50)

WHERE TO GO

FIUMARA D'ARTE ●

(139 E2) (*𝄞 H3–4*)

Fiumara di Tusa, the beach at *Villa Margi* and *Castel di Lucio* with its maze are an open-air museum of modern scultpure. Artists also designed the rooms of the avant-garde hotel *Atelier sul Mare* (44 rooms | tel. 09 21 33 42 95 | www.atelier sulmare.com | *Moderate–Expensive*) in the coastal village *Castel di Tusa* (32 km/20 miles east of Cefalù). The hotel's website guides you to nine sculptures in the countryside with links to Google Maps. ◕ *Agriturismo Casa Migliaca (tel. 09 21 33 67 22 | www.casamigliaca.com | Moderate, restaurant Budget)* is located on a hill above the Fiumara di Tusa valley near *Pettineo*. The 17th-century manor house has 8 rooms; the food (residents only) comes from its own organic production. Colourful ceramics are made in ● *Santo Stefano di Camastra*. Most shops display their wares on the road.

LE MADONIE ⭐
(138–139 C–E2) (𝄚 G–H4)
You can get to know the Madonie Mountains by taking this circular tour (approx. 145 km/90 miles). The *pilgrimage church in Gibilmanna* is in a holm oak wood on the edge of the mountains. Refreshing springs and paths for hiking and riding attract lots of people from the towns at weekends. There are also a number of good trattorias in the villages as well as places that sell cheese, local cold meats, farmhouse bread, olive oil and wine. Accommodation is available in mountain cabins and on farms *(agriturismo)*.
The mountain village INSIDER TIP *Isnello* is the gateway to what is Sicily's most important skiing area after Mount Etna. Mountain hikes of all degrees of difficulty can be made from spring until late autumn. *Piano Zucchi* (1105 m/3625 ft) and *Piano Battaglia* (1500 m/4920 ft), which both have cabins of the Club Alpino Siciliano (CAS), are the best starting points. Just below, in a restored country house, is the *Piano Torre* hotel (26

rooms | tel. 0 92 16 26 71 | *Moderate*) with a pool and good restaurant.
The intimate, child-friendly ● INSIDER TIP *Agriturismo Gelso (4 rooms | Loc. Catalani | tel. 09 21 64 23 10 | www.agriturismogel so.it | Budget)* is surrounded by almond groves in Castellana Sicula. It offers cookery classes and a small ◕ trattoria serving excellent regional dishes from homegrown ingredients.
From Petralia head east to *Gangi* (pop. 7000) where the closely built houses cover the mountain like a hat. The labyrinth of narrow streets can only be explored on foot.
Now drive back 9 km (5½ miles) to Bivio Geraci and, from there, up to *Geraci Siculo* that lies 1077 m (3530 ft) above sea level. One of the most far-reaching views over

---

⭐ **Duomo di Cefalù**
The fortress-like building can be seen from afar → **p. 61**

⭐ **Le Madonie**
Beautiful scenery and lovely mountain villages → **p. 63**

⭐ **Palazzo dei Normanni and Cappella Palatina**
Byzantines and Arabs created this royal palace → **p. 67**

⭐ **Street markets**
Colourful, loud and lively: the markets in Palermo → **p. 68**

⭐ **Monreale Cathedral**
One of the greatest examples of Norman architecture → **p. 71**

⭐ **Monte Pellegrino**
A bird's-eye view of Palermo → **p. 71**

MARCO POLO HIGHLIGHTS

Sicily is the reward for taking a walk through the narrow streets to the church and the ruins of the castle above the village. On a clear day, Etna, 75 km (46 miles) away, looms like a giant above the barren mountainous countryside of central Sicily. There is always a lot going on at the entrance to the village around the old *village fountain* of pink stone. Locals come here to fill up their bottles and canisters with mineral water from a nearby spring.

A twisty mountain road leads for 23 km (14 miles) through cork oak woods to *Castelbuono* (pop. 8900). The entrance to the Old Town is guarded by the well-preserved castle with its impressive courtyard, a museum exhibiting works by classical modern Italian painters, and the *Cappella Sant'Anna,* a masterpiece of Baroque stucco art *(daily 9/10am–1/1.30pm and 3.30/4.30pm–7.30/8pm | admission 4 euros | www.museocivico.eu).* The natural history museum, the *Museo Minà Palumbo (Mon–Sat 9am–1pm, 3pm–7pm | Via Roma 52 | admission 2 euros | www.museominapalumbo.it)*, is the life's work of the scientist Francesco Minà Palumbo, who walked the Madonie Mountains time and again in the 19th century. The showcases display fossils, butterflies, hand-drawn and coloured sheets of plants, archeological finds and stuffed birds. INSIDER TIP *Nangalarruni (closed Wed | Via delle Confraternità 5 | tel. 09 21 67 14 28 | www.hostarianangalarruni.it | Moderate)* serves excellent mushrooms. The *Fiasconaro* bar on the *piazza* has the best *panettone* south of Milan.

PALERMO

MAP INSIDE BACK COVER
(138 B1) *(E3)* **The location of Palermo (pop. 669,000) in the Conca d'Oro – "the Golden Shell"–, framed by the mountains behind Monreale and Monte Pellegrino, is magnificent. In the 18th century the setting was even described as "the most beautiful in the world".**

Even today, the most evocative way to approach Palermo is by ship. First you catch a glimpse of the theatrical mountains on the north coast before entering the bay, where the towers and domes become increasingly clear. The centre of this, one of the most magnificent cities of palaces in Europe 200 years ago, is frequently a jolting juxtaposition of mafia-like neglect and exuberant vitality – particularly on the colourful, exotic markets. Parts of the Old Town are in ruins, swathes of destruction where World War II bombs and subsequent speculation have torn holes in the city's fabric. Other streets are so full of people from dawn until well into the night that you can hardly make headway. Life is gradually coming back to Europe's capital of culture of 2018. Restoration work and building is going on everywhere; committed young people are moving back into the Old Town. Shops, pubs and places to meet are opening up on every corner.

As everywhere in Sicily, the dominant ar-

> CITY **WHERE TO START?**
> **Centre:** Palermo's centre and the Old Town stretch around the inner-city bay La Cala. By car, simply follow signs to the harbour (*porto*) where you can find somewhere to park in the Via Crispi or in the roads behind (pay and display). Take the Via Crispi and you'll find yourself in the middle of Old Palermo. From the station *(Stazione Centrale)*, which is also where most coaches stop, the Via Roma leads directly through the centre.

chitectural style is Baroque. The magnificence of the Norman buildings and mosaics stopped later generations from demolishing, remodelling or covering them up. There is nothing left from earlier eras – of the hundreds of houses of worship and mosques constructed by the Arabs in what in the 10th century was the largest city in Europe. Nevertheless, early Norman churches such as *San Giovanni degli Eremiti* and *San Cataldo* as well as to two garden palaces *La Cuba* and *La Zisa* give some impression of the Arabian influence in Sicily.

SIGHTSEEING

CATTEDRALE
Only the dimensions of the cathedral and the Norman style of the unaltered choir are remnants of when the building was erected (1185). The impressive Late Gothic side façade with the main portico is of Catalan influence; the dome and the interior are from the late 18th century – very austere. Inside, the polished porphyry sarcophagi of Frederick II (1194–1250) and other members of the royal and imperial families can be seen. *Cathedral Mon–Sat 9am–7pm, Sun 8am–1pm and 4–7pm, royal tombs Mon–Sat 9am–5.30pm, Sun 10am–1pm | admission 1.50 euros*

CONVENTO DEI CAPPUCCINI
A spooky and macabre experience (not at all suitable for children!) which throws light on Sicilian piety and *memento mori* (reminder of death): The Capuchin friars and members of the aristocracy had themselves mummified. Covered with dust and dressed in clothes that have become cocoons, they remain preserved in the monastery catacombs. In centuries past they were even dressed in new fashionable clothes from time to time. *Daily 9am–1pm and 3pm–6pm | admission 3 euros*

Palermo Cathedral, the burial place of royal and imperial families

ECOMUSEO MARE MEMORIA VIVA
Industrial architecture meets video installations. Photos and perspectives of the capital Palermo are on display under the iron girders of this locomotive shed built in 1886. *Tue–Sun 9am–6.30pm | Via Messina Marinare 27 | admission free | www.marememoriaviva.it*

GALLERIA D'ARTE MODERNA (GAM)
Art from between 1800 and 1900. An excellent collection of works, also by Sicilian artists, is displayed in the beautifully restored former monastery of *Santa Anna alla Kalsa. Tue–Sun 9.30am–6.30pm | Via Sant'Anna 21 | admission 7 euros*

GALLERIA REGIONALE DELLA SICILIA
Housed in the Gothic Catalan *Palazzo Abatellis,* the museum showcases Sicily's artistic past including the bust of Eleonora d'Aragon by Francesco Laurana, the head of a boy by Antonello Gagini, and paint-

ings on panel such as **INSIDER TIP** Antonello da Messina's "Annunciation". The film-maker Wim Wenders once commented that this small picture was "more beautiful and magical than the Mona Lisa." *Tue–Fri 9am–6pm, Sat/Sun 9am–1pm | Via Alloro 4 | admission 8 euros*

LA KALSA

Al-Halisah, "the Chosen One", is the name the Arabs gave this district on the shore and around the harbour. It was here that the palace of the Caliphs once stood. Later, the nobility built palaces and churches here, enjoyed an evening walk around the *Porta Felice* and along the sea where, today, there are lots of stalls selling fish and ice cream. There is a wonderful view of the coastline and the Old Town from the ❧ *Passeggiata delle Cattive,* that runs along the city walls past the mighty Palazzo Butera. Following air raids in 1943, the district suffered from depopulation as a result of the Mafia and speculation. However, in the past few years, La Kalsa has experienced a revival. The *Piazza Marina* with its huge 200-year-old rubber trees and masses of trattorias is lively well into the night. Lots of restoration work is going on in the main streets, *Via Alloro* and *Via Torremuzza*, lined with tall Baroque palaces and churches.

The façade of *San Francesco d'Assisi*, with its richly decorated rose window, is impressive. The Gothic hall church is one of the few medieval churches in Palermo without any Baroque embellishments. The life-sized plasterwork allegories of virtues and vices by Giacomo Serpotta of 1723 provide a stark contrast. A visit to *Palazzo Mirto (Tue–Sat 9am–6pm, Sun 9am–1pm | Via Merlo 2 | admission 6 euros)* provides a glimpse of upper-class life in the 18th-century. *La Magione (daily 9am–7pm, in winter Sun 9am–1pm only | admission 2 euros)*, a plain Norman church with an enchanting cloister, borders large open areas in this part of La Kalsa that was never rebuilt after the war.

LA MARTORANA AND SAN CATALDO

The two churches stand on a small hillock not far from the *Piazza Pretoria.* No ornamentation distracts from the plain stone structure of *San Cataldo* with its a tall red domes that has been so well preserved. The bell tower of *La Martorana* with its delicate-looking columns and pointed arched windows became the template for many Norman churches including several in the south of mainland Italy. The interior is covered in golden mosaics by Byzantine master craftsmen. *Mon–Sat 9.30am–1pm and 3.30pm–5.30pm, Sun 9am–10.30am (La Martorana); daily 9.30am–12.30pm and 3–6pm (San Cataldo) | admission 2 euros (La Martorana), 2.50 euros (San Cataldo)*

MUSEO ARCHEOLOGICO

The museum is housed in a former monastery. Burial stelae and sarcophagi are displayed in the Renaissance cloister. The ancient metopes (reliefs on a temple frieze) from Selinunt are exceptional examples of Greek sculpture. *Tue–Sat 9.30am–6.30pm, Sun 9.30am–1pm | Piazza Olivella 24 | admission free*

INSIDER TIP ORTO BOTANICO ●

Laid out as a pleasure garden in 1792 for the upper classes, the garden today is a shady paradise with huge trees from both the Mediterranean and the Tropics. It provides an extensive overview of the regional flora and those plants from all over the world that have become established here. *March/Oct daily 9am–6pm, April/Sept daily 9am–7pm, May–Aug daily 9am–8pm, Nov–Feb daily 9am–5pm | Via Lincoln 2 | admission 5 euros | www.ortobotanico.unipa.it*

PALAZZO DEI NORMANNI AND CAPPELLA PALATINA ★

The former *royal palace*, the origins of which date back to the 9th century, has been the seat of the regional government of Sicily and regional parliament since 1947. The *cappella*, the royal chapel, was embellished by Arab, Norman and Byzantine artists. The interior is completely covered with gold mosaics and marble intarsia, the former being the work of artists from Constantinople. The chancel contains King Roger II's (Ruggero's) coronation throne with rich intarsia work, the Easter candlestick, the ambon used as a pulpit and the high altar. The wooden "stalactite" ceiling, which can now be seen in all its colourful magnificence following its restoration, looks as if it has come out of an Oriental fairytale. The entrance is outside the city wall. *Mon–Sat 8.15am–5.40pm, Sun 8.15am–1pm (not during mass 9.45am–11.15am), last admission 5pm/12.15pm | Piazza Indipendenza | admission Tue–Thu 7, Fri–Mon 8.50 euros | tel. for reservations 09 16 26 28 33 | www.ars.sicilia.it | www.federicosecundo.org*

SAN GIOVANNI DEGLI EREMITI

In the garden of the former monastery church below the Norman palace, the sound of water, the palm trees and exotic plants give a very good idea of the opulence of oriental Palermo and the Arab-influenced lifestyle led by the privileged in Norman times. *Tue–Sat 9am–7pm, Sun/Mon 9am–1.30pm | admission 6 euros*

TEATRO MASSIMO ●

This theatre staged the premiere of Puccini's masterpiece "La Bohème". A temple for opera fans and known among cinema goers from the bloody finale of "Godfather III". Built 1875–97 by the Palermo-born Giovan B. Basile. The *Caffè del Teatro (daily 10am–11pm) is a hidden gem. Opera season Nov–May, guided tours daily 9.30am–6pm | Piazza Verdi | 8 euros | www.teatromassimo.it*

VIA VALVERDE ORATORIES AND CHURCHES

Just a few yards apart, hidden behind the massive Baroque church of San Domenico, are a number of small Baroque churches and oratories. *Oratorio del Rosario* and *Oratorio di Santa Cita* contain exceptionally life-like plasterwork figures and reliefs by the Baroque artist Giacomo Serpotta; the churches *Santa Cita, Santa Maria in Valverde* and *San Giorgio dei Genovesi* have an unusual number of paintings, marble statues and stone intarsia work. *Daily*

The impressive *ficus macrophylla* with aerial roots in the botanical garden

9am–6pm | admission 6 euros | www.il
geniodipalermo.com

INSIDER TIP LA ZISA

In the 12th century, Arabian builders
erected this royal summer residence. The
tall cube is elegantly subdivided by decorative arches, windows and portals. The
fountain niche, with its delicate pendant
arches, from which the water flows outside, can be seen in the imposing hall
decorated with mosaic friezes and marble
tiles. Concealed flues, clay pipes and running water create a form of air condition-
ing that still works 800 years on. *Mon–
Sat 9am–7pm, Sun 9am–1.30pm |
admission 6 euros*

FOOD & DRINK

ANTICA FOCACCERIA S. FRANCESCO ◐

From nose to tail – nothing new for
Palermo locals but a gourmet sensation
for everyone else. If you've never tried
"bread with spleen" *(pani ca meusa)*, sea-
soned with organic lemon and sheep's
ricotta, then you haven't tasted authen-
tic Sicilian cuisine yet. *Daily | Via A. Pater-
nostro 58 | tel. 0 91 32 02 64 | www.anti
cafocacceria.it | Budget*

BISSO BISTROT

This hotspot in Quattro Canti attracts
both travellers and young Palermo locals
for their breakfast cornettoes or to try
pasta with wild fennel. *Closed Sun | Via
Maqueda 172 | mobile tel. 32 81 31 45 95 |
Budget–Moderate*

INSIDER TIP FUD ◐

Fud = food, get it? The Big Mac was
yesterday: here they celebrate the tri-
umph of the regional burger with don-
key or buffalo mincemeat. A casually
cool location. (Another branch in Cat-
ania, Via S. Filomena 35.) *Daily | Piaz-

za Olivella 4 | tel. 09 16 11 21 84 | www.
fud.it | Budget*

INSIDER TIP IL MIRTO E LA ROSA ◐

Fresh seasonal produce, lots of vegetar-
ian, gluten-free, seafood and a few meat
dishes from naturally reared animals,
exquisite desserts. *Via Principe di
Granatelli 30 | tel. 0 91 32 53 53 | www.
ilmirtoelarosa.com | Moderate*

TRATTORIA IL BERSAGLIERE

No telefono, no wifi, no english, no
menu, no tourists: tiny, narrow restaurant with paper tablecloths, pic-
tures of the Madonna and neon lights.
The Battaglia family has been cooking here for Palermo locals since 1904.
*Closed Sun and evenings | Via S. Nicolo
all´Alberghiera 38 | Budget*

SHOPPING

CRAFT SHOPS

The district between the *station*, *Via
Roma, Piazza Cassa di Risparmio, Piazza
Rivoluzione* and *Via Garibaldi* is a piece of
"Old Palermo" with craftspeople such as
milliners, tailors and candlemakers.

LA COPPOLA STORTA ●

This is where you can buy a genuine
Sicilian *coppola* from San Giuseppe Jato,
in any number of colours, for men, wom-
en and children, made of coarse or soft
material, and for every conceivable occasion. And just to rid any doubt as to
who wears this cap today: the shop is on
the "Addio pizzo" list. *Via Bara all'Olivella
74*

STREET MARKETS ★ ●

There are several famous food markets
in the Old Town. And, after a lengthy mid-
day break, many standholders keep going well into the evening. The largest

Catch of the day from the Mediterranean on display at the Capo district market

market in the Capo district is held around Sant'Agostino church and stretches down several roads as far as the Teatro Massimo; the ● *Ballaró market* caters for the area around Porta Sant'Antonio, the Chiesa del Carmine and Chiesa del Gesù. The big *non-food market*, consisting largely of clothing and household wares, sprawls from Piazza San Domenico to Piazza Papireto.

ENTERTAINMENT

Palermo, once known for its eerily quiet streets in the evenings because of the Mafiosi, has emerged as a party destination. Hotspots include the district around *Teatro Massimo,* the pedestrian zone of *Via Maqueda* and the *seafront promenade* with its eye-catching *Nautoscopio (Piazzetta Capitaneria del Porto),* a crow's nest which is used as a concert stage.

BERLIN CAFÈ

This overcrowded cocktail bar serving, among other drinks, German beer, is a popular cosmopolitan haunt for Paler-mo's over-thirty clientele. *Daily 6pm–2am | Via Isidoro La Lumia 19–21*

WHERE TO STAY

CENTRALE PALACE

The small one among the historical grand hotels. Very centrally located in a palazzo adorned with frescos. Pretty roof terrace. *104 rooms | Corso Vittorio Emanuele 327 | tel. 09 18 53 9 | www.centralepalacehotel. it | Expensive*

LA FUITINA

Tiny oasis in the noisy old town centre. Three rooms, chandeliers and common kitchen inside a Baroque palazzo near the Vucciria market. *Via Garraffello 6 | tel. 09 19 76 65 01 | Budget*

JOLI

Stylish turn-of-the-century building on the Piazza Ignazio Florio with bold colours and wall and ceiling frescos. Roof terrace. *30 rooms | Via Michele Amari 11 | tel. 09 16 11 17 65 | www.hoteljoli.com | Moderate*

AAPIT (Piazza Castelnuovo 34 | tel. 09 16 05 838 47 | www.palermotourism.com | www.palermoweb.com)

WHERE TO GO

BAGHERIA (138 B1) (*ω F3*)

In the 18th and 19th centuries, the splendid villas and parks of the aristocratic families could be found close to this now concrete-covered town (pop. 54,000), 16 km (10 miles) east of Palermo. The *Villa Palagonia (daily 9am–1pm, April–Oct 3.30pm–6.30pm, Nov–March 3.30pm–5.30pm | admission 6 euros | www.villapalagonia.it)*, with its array of sculpted monsters and gnomes in the garden, its hall of mirrors and the frescos of the Labours of Hercules inside aroused the curiosity of illustrious travellers. The works of the Neorealist painter Renato Guttuso (1911–87), born in Bagheria, are displayed at the INSIDER TIP *Galleria d'Arte Moderna* in the *Villa Cattolica (Tue–Sun 9am–5pm | admission 5 euros | www.museoguttuso.com)*

LOW BUDGET

Cortese (26 rooms | Via Scarparelli 16 | tel. 09 133 17 22 | www.hotelcortese. info), a clean hotel popular among young tourists, is located in the liveliest part of Palermo's Old Town.

Explore Palermo by bus: you have the choice between a normal bus ticket valid for 1½ hours (1.40 euros/1.80 on the bus) and day tickets (1 to 7 days; 1 day 3.50 euros, 7 days 16.80 euros). Tickets also sold in tabacchi shops. *www.amat.pa.it*

alongside those of other 20th-century Sicilian artists. *Trattoria Don Ciccio (closed Wed, Sun and in August | Via del Cavaliere 87 | tel. 0 91 93 24 42 | Budget)* serves good old fashioned fare.

CORLEONE (138 B3) (*ω E4*)

This small town (pop. 11,000), the home of bosses and godfathers, crops up in virtually every Mafia novel and film, as well as in daily reports in the press and on television, even though the "Corleonesi" didn't actually reach any positions of power within the Mafia through bloody means until they were in Palermo. In the ⊕ INSIDER TIP *CIDMA (guided tours Mon–Fri 10am/11am/noon/3pm/4pm/5pm | admission 5–15 euros, depending on number of participants | pre-booking recommended: tel. 0 91 84 52 42 95 | Via G. Valenti 7 | www.cidmacorleone.it)* in the old town centre, once in the ownership of the former superboss Provenzano and impounded by the State, photos and documents about the Mafia and the struggle against the godfathers can be seen. Produce and wine grown on land seized from Mafia clans is also sold here. The craggy bastion, the INSIDER TIP *Rocca Busambra*, lies 1613 m (4318 ft) above sea level in barren hilly country. The mountain forests, caves and clefts in this karst landscape provided perfect hiding and burial places for the Mafia. Some of these can be reached along marked trails which start at *Bosco di Ficuzza,* the former hunting lodge of Bourbon kings. Accommodation and good food is available at *Alpe Cucco (18 rooms | 70 beds | mobile tel. 33 13 98 79 53 | www.alpecucco.it | Budget)*, a mountain hut reached by car at an altitude of just under 1000 m/3280 ft.

MONDELLO (138 B1) (*ω E3*)

Palermo's beach is 15 km (9½ miles) from the city, protected from the worst of the

Heaven on earth: the golden mosaics in Monreale Cathedral

pollution by Monte Pellegrino. Some of the Art Nouveau villas with their beautiful gardens have not yet been hemmed in by concrete blocks. The hotel *Conchiglia d'Oro (50 rooms | tel. 0 91 45 03 59 | www. hotelconchigliadoro.it | Moderate)* is on a quiet side road. The restaurant *Bye Bye Blues (closed Sun evenings and Mon | Via Garofalo 23 | tel. 09 16 84 14 15 | www. byebyeblues.it | Moderate)* has excellent seafood.

MONREALE (138 B1) (*Ш E3*)

The ★ *Cathedral of Monreale (April–Oct daily 8.30am–12.30pm (Sun 8am–9.15am) and 2.30–4.45pm, Nov–March daily 8.30am–12.45pm (Sun 9.30am–9.30am) and 3–4.30/5pm | admission 4 euros)* 8 km/5 miles west of Palermo was founded as a Benedictine monastery in 1174 under the Normans and granted a huge area of land throughout western Sicily. It is the largest and most compact ecclesiastical building of that era. Inside, approached through two Roman bronze doors, the walls are covered in golden mosaics covering 68,250ft². For some, it's the eighth wonder of the world! The flora and fauna ornamentation on the 228 capitals in the cloister *(Mon–Sat 9am–6.30pm, Sun 9am–1pm | admission 6 euros)*, with a garden and fountains, introduces a natural element into the secluded world of the monastery. The B&B *Elvira al Duomo (3 rooms | Via S. Liberata 17 | tel. 09 16 40 71 65 | www. elviraduomo.it | Budget)* is known for its pretty garden and friendliness. Sicilian country fare and steaks near the cathedral square in *Bricco & Bracco (closed Mon | Via D'Acquisto 13 | tel. 09 16 41 77 73 | www.briccoebrracco.it | Moderate)*.

MONTE PELLEGRINO ★ ☀
(138 B1) (*Ш E3*)

Palermo's "own" thickly wooded mountain is 13 km (8 miles) from the city and 606 m (1990 ft) high, and offers a fantastic view over the city and the Conca d'Oro. The *pilgrimage church dedicated to St Rosalia,* the patron saint of Palermo, is built in a natural cave.

THE SOUTHWEST

The west and the south coast between Gela and Selinunte are largely untouched by tourism. Only not-to-be-missed sites such as the Greek temples in Agrigento, Selinunte and Segesta experience hordes of visitors. Here, more than any other place on Sicily, you will experience the island's vastness and exposure to the natural elements of sun, wind and rain.

To the north between Trapani and Alcamo, bare mountains mark the boundary of the expansive plains with their salt works and endless vineyards stretching as far as Marsala and Selinunte on the south coast. This links up with an also seemingly endless expanse of undulating hilly countryside with wide valleys and villages perched on mountain tops. Following the brief but intense period in early summer when pop-

pies and gorse blossom and fields of crops turn red and yellow, the virtually treeless ground becomes scorched, its sparse woodland having fallen victim to the axe more than 2000 years ago.

AGRIGENTO

(138 C5) (*ꟿ F6*) The ancient city of Akragas, the medieval Girgenti and the Agrigento of the past 30 years are three towns that, unlike other places in Sicily, are not built one on top of the other.
Each has its own site, even if the high-rises in new Agrigento (pop. 60,000) partially block the view of Old Girgenti and the city from Antiquity in the *Valle dei Templi*.

From the obligatory tours of ancient sites to
unchartered tourist territory: ruined temples,
endless vineyards and bizarre rock formations

SIGHTSEEING

OLD TOWN

The urban centre is the *Piazzale Aldo Moro*
with its many palm trees that links the
medieval part with the modern town. Both
from here and the ☀️ park along the
Viale della Vittoria you have a fantastic
panoramic view across the Valley of the
Temples and the sea.

On the *Via Atenea*, take the first flight of
steps – that are so typical of Girgenti – up
to the church of *Santo Spirito*. In the

Chiesa del Purgatorio on Via Atenea there
is a splendid INSIDER TIP cycle of figures
of the virtues by Giacomo Serpotta (care-
taker in courtyard). The *Cattedrale di San
Gerlando* (in danger of collapsing) is on
the highest point of the Old Town. Its
large interior with octagonal pillars and
richly carved coffered ceiling is impressive.

MUSEO ARCHEOLOGICO REGIONALE

Finds from ancient Akragas and the early
culture of various peoples in the centre
of Sicily. A model of the 7.75 m (25½ ft)

These columns in the Temple of Heracles are more than 10 m (33 ft) high

VALLE DEI TEMPLI ★

The ancient city and its temples lie hidden among well-tended almond and olive groves. Start your tour from the centre of the plateau *Collina dei Templi (daily 8.30am–7pm | admission 10 euros, incl. museum 13.50 euros | www.distrettotu risticodelleminiere.it)* taking the usual approach along road no. 118. To the left, a path leads up to the piles of stones of the *Temple of Heracles* of which 8 columns are still standing. You then have an unrestricted view of the impressively symmetrical *Temple of Concorde* from the 5th century BC. Its exceptional condition is due to its conversion into a Christian church in the 6th century. After taking the path to the *Temple of Juno*, which has half its original columns still standing, located at the highest point of ancient Akragas, walk directly above the steep drop and look down on the *Tomb of Theron*.

Returning to the car park, you enter the archeological zone. The *Temple of Olympian Zeus* is a pile of huge blocks of stone and column drums. Building work started following the victory over the Carthaginians at Himera in 480 BC. With a length of 112m (367 ft) and a width of 58 m (190 ft), it was one of the largest temples in Antiquity. The Carthaginians destroyed the incomplete building in 406 BC and it was later further damaged by an earthquake. At the far boundary of the lower level with remains of a holy site, is the *Sanctuary of the Chtonic Gods (Tempio delle divinità chtonie)* with sacrificial pits and the *Temple of Castor and Pollux*. A path leads down to the INSIDER TIP *Giardino della Kolymbetra (daily 9.30am–5.30/6.30/7.30pm, in winter 10am–2pm | admission 6 euros),* a natural paradise with orange groves, almond and olive treees. Galleries in the sandstone walls lead to subterranean

high telamon from the Temple of Zeus can be seen in one of the rooms. The Romanesque monastery church of *San Nicola*, where the Phaedra sarcophagus from Late Antiquity depicting the tragic love of Phaedra and her stepson Hippolytus can be seen, also belongs to the museum. *Tue–Sat 9am–7.30pm, Sun/Mon 9am–1pm | admission 8 euros, incl. excavations 13.50 euros*

springs whose water was used to irrigate the valley and for fish farming.

Don't forget to take plenty of water with you as well as some *panini* and fruit for a picnic if you visit the very extensive and sunny *Zona Archeologica*. Eating out in the Valle dei Templi, regardless of the restaurant category, is one of the worst in Sicily with regard to value for money.

FOOD & DRINK

DA CARMELO

Snails, rabbit, lamb and kid are served in this village trattoria. *Thu–Tue evenings only, Sun also lunch | Via Roma 16 | Joppolo Giancaxio | 12 km (7½ miles) north | tel. 09 22 63 13 76 | Budget*

KOKALOS

Travel groups are attracted to this restaurant's pretty garden with views of the temple. Pizzas from the wood-fired oven in the evenings. *Daily | Via Alfredo Capitano 3 | tel. 09 22 60 64 27 | www.ristorante-kokalos.net | Budget*

WHERE TO STAY

AGRITURISMO FATTORIA MOSÈ ☺

Friendly 17th-century manor house and organic farm, garden and museum. *8 flats | Villaggio Mosè | Via Mattia Pascal 4a | tel. 09 22 60 61 15 | www.fattoria mose.com | Moderate*

VILLA ATHENA

Evenings around the pool with views up to the illuminated Concordia temple. Romantic five-star luxury in a completely refurbished baronial palace from the 18th century. *27 rooms | Via Passeggiata Archeologica 33 | tel. 09 22 59 62 88 | www.hotelvillaathena.it | Expensive*

VILLA CETTA (138 C6) (*ᗯ F6*)

B & B with garden on the beach in San Leone. *2 rooms | Via Giovanni Fattori 9 | tel. 09 22 416452 | www.villacetta.it | Budget–Moderate*

INFORMATION

Servizio Turistico Regionale (Via Empedocle 73 | tel. 0 92 22 03 91)

WHERE TO GO

INSIDER TIP **CAMPOBELLO DI LICATA (139 D6) (*ᗯ G6*)**

Since 1980, the Argentinian artist Silvio Benedetto has been designing squares, decorating façades with murals, sculpting and creating wall and floor mosaics in this former mining town (pop. 10,000). In the

---

MARCO POLO HIGHLIGHTS

★ **Valle dei Templi**
Antiquity in its entirety: a whole valley of Greek temples → p. 74

★ **Gibellina**
A centre of modern architecture → p. 78

★ **Selinunte**
Greek temples above the sea → p. 79

★ **Eraclea Minoa**
A magical ancient site above the snow-white chalk cliffs → p. 80

★ **Erice**
A perfectly preserved, small medieval town → p. 83

★ **Segesta**
A Greek temple and theatre in solitary mountains → p. 85

Valle delle Pietre dipinte (in the summer Tue–Sun 9am–1pm, 4pm–8pm | free admission), characters and scenes from Dante's *Divine Comedy* have been depicted on 110 travertine slabs. Scenes and figures from Homer's *Iliad* on 24 ceramic tiles create one large image (7 × 3 m, 23 × 10 ft) in the auditorium. Further information: *www.comune.campobellodi licata.ag.it* and *www.silviobenedetto.com*

GELA (142 A4) (*m* H7)

This industrial town (pop. 75,000) 78 km (48½ miles) east of Agrigento is worth a detour to see the Greek town walls at *Capo Soprano*. In keeping with Gela's importance in Antiquity, the *Museo Regionale Archeologico (Mon–Sat 9am– 7pm | admission 4 euros)* next to the Parco Rimembranza boasts a number of valuable finds and a remarkable coin collection. The ● trattoria *San Giovanni (closed Sun | Via Damaggio Fischetti 51 | tel. 09 33 91 26 74 | Budget)* offers a young regional cuisine and a delicious *caponata*. The beach in *Falconara*, 20 km (12½ miles) towards Agrigento, with a castle in the background, is lovely.

LOW BUDGET

Unrefined sea salt from the *Ettore Infersa* pits on Mozia makes a nice souvenir – the packaging alone is a delight *(to the west of the Marsala–Birgi road | www.salineettoreinfe rsa.com)*.

The *Rosticceria Palumbo (Piazza Pirandello 26 | tel. 0 92 22 97 65)* in Agrigento sells roast chicken with rosemary, rice arancini or antipasti to take-away or eat in its snack bar.

PALMA DI MONTECHIARO
(138 C6) (*m* F6)

The family of the novelist Giuseppe Tomasi di Lampedusa originated from this town 24 km (15 miles) east of Agrigento. *Marina di Palma* is just 4 km (2½ miles) away where the cliffs are dominated by a ruined castle. One of the most creative cuisines in Sicily, INSIDER TIP *La Madia (closed Tue, Sun evenings | Via Filippo Re 22 | tel. 09 22 77 14 43 | www.ristorantelamadia. it | Expensive)*, can be found in the port of *Licata* 18 km (11 miles) away. Those who want to spend less try the *"poesia di terra e di mare"* by Peppe Bonsignore at *L'Oste e il Sacrestano (closed Sun evening and Mon | Via S. Andrea 19 | tel. 09 22 77 46 36 | Moderate)*.

REALMONTE AND SICULIANA
(138 B5) (*m* E6)

Between Porto Empedocle and Sciacca the main road runs 3–8 km (2–5 miles) inland from the coast with smaller roads leading off to secluded beaches. Near Realmonte, snow-white sandstone cliffs at *Capo Rosello* drop 90 m/295 ft into the sea below. Apart from a rocky coastline, *Siculiana Marina* has a flat sandy beach that stretches to the west as far as Torre Salsa.
La Scogliera (closed Sun evening and Mon | tel. 09 22 81 75 32 | Moderate) on the promenade along the shore serves good seafood. Accommodation is available in holiday flats and in the hotel *Paguro Residence (12 rooms | tel. 09 22 81 55 10 | www.hotel-residencepaguro.it | Budget–Moderate)* in the town above the beach. The INSIDER TIP dunes at *Torre Salsa* line the 6 km (4 miles) long beach and form part of the WWF nature reserve that covers 1880 acres *(entrance at the visitor centre | tel. 09 22 81 82 20 | www.wwftorresalsa.it)*. The agriturismo farm *Torre Salsa (13 flats | tel. 09 22 84 70 74 | www.torresalsa.it |*

Moderate) is located behind the dunes and rents out "Southern Walking" poles.

MARSALA

(136 C4) (📖 B4) Towards the west, Sicily flattens out before running into the sea. *Capo Lilibeo*, the most westerly point of the island, is part of the town of Marsala (pop. 83,000). Marsala is the marketing and wine centre of western Sicily.

John Woodhouse is to be thanked for this role. While under Napoleonic rule, he created Marsala fortified wine as a substitute for the much loved port so missed by the English. You can try and buy it in many wine cellars in the town.

SIGHTSEEING

OLD TOWN

The pretty Baroque town lies inside the largely intact 16th-century town walls. The *Piazza della Repubblica* is the town's front room with arcades and loggias, a fountain in the middle and the cathedral of *San Tommaso*. The foundations of a Roman settlement are beyond *Porta Nuova*.

CANTINA MARCO DE BARTOLI ● 🌿

The former racing driver Marco de Bartoli is seen as the pioneer of the new dry Marsala wine and pure wine made from autochthonous, traditional grape varieties. You can taste his oenological heritage on an enjoyable 60 to 90-minute tour. *Mon–Fri, approx. 10am and 3pm | Contrada Samperi | pre-booking tel. 09 23 96 20 93 | 15–20 euros | www.marcodebartoli.com*

MUSEO ARCHEOLOGICO BAGLIO ANSELMI

The remains of a Punic ship from the 3rd century BC that was raised in 1969 off

It will be some time before these grapes are made into wine

Marsala can be seen here. Also includes finds from the Punic and Roman settlement. *Sun–Tue 9am–12.30pm, Wed–Sat 9am–5.30pm | on Capo Lilibeo | admission 4 euros*

FOOD & DRINK

IL GALLO E L'INNAMORATA

Fish rice arancini or tuna in mint sauce are served in this osteria in the old town. *Closed Mon | Via Stefano Bilardello 18 | tel. 0 92 31 95 44 46 | Moderate*

WHERE TO STAY

IL PROFUMO DEL SALE 🌿

In her "the smell of salt" B&B, Ligurian Celsa Carissimi rents out three brightly furnished rooms and offers tips on slow-food tours. *Via Vaccari 8 | tel. 0 92 31 89 04 72 | www.ilprofumodelsale.it | Budget*

WHERE TO GO

GIBELLINA ⭐ (137 E4) (*∅ D4*)

Following the earthquake in 1968, temporary shelters were built in Belice Valley that threatened to become a permanent feature. Government funding was diverted into the pockets of the Mafia and corrupt politicians. Gibellina had been devastated and the demoralised residents struggled as more and more people left. They demonstrated in Rome and invited not only politicians to visit them but also artists who drew attention to Gibellina and reconstruction efforts. The old village is a sea of debris, partly overgrown and partly a concrete monument. Alberto Burri's *Cretto* is continuously growing and is thought to be the largest work of land art in Europe with regard to the area it covers. The new settlement is 20 km (12½ miles) away. It is an urban experiment with remarkable modern architectural designs and a pleasant and spaciously laid-out residential landscape with gardens, which is, in part, already

deteriorating again. In the *Museo delle Trame Mediterranee (Tue–Sun 9am–1pm, 3pm–6pm | admission 5 euros | www.fon dazioneorestiadi.it)* in Baglio di Stefano just outside the town, works by classical modernist and contemporary artists (Joseph Beuys, Giorgio de Chirico, Pietro Consagra, Renato Guttuso), delicate jewellery, ceramics and sumptuous garments largely from North Africa and the Orient are on display. The *Museo d'Arte Contemporanea* boasts the largest collection of modern art in Sicily, comprising 1800 paintings, statues and objects. Village life before the earthquake is documented in the ethnological section which focuses on old professions and equipment. Couscous and pizza are being served at *Ristorante Massara (closed Tue | Via Vespri Siciliani 29 | tel. 0 92 46 78 71 | Budget–Moderate)*. B & B *Gibellina Arte (Via Empedocle 16 | tel. 0 92 46 76 97 | www. gibellinarte.it | Budget)* has 6 rooms and a kitchen for guests.

The large ● INSIDER TIP spa *Terme di Acqua Pia (in summer daily 9am–mid-*

Gibellina under cement: the monumental memorial "Cretto" by Alberto Burri

night | admission 10–15 euros | tel. 0 92 53 90 26 | www.termeacquapia.it) is situated on the road to Montevago (20 km/12½ miles southeast) with a pool, spa area, hot springs, park, restaurant *(Budget)* and guest accommodation *(26 rooms, 3 flats | Budget–Expensive)*.

MAZARA DEL VALLO (136 C4) *(ﾛ C5)*

Italy's largest fishing port 22 km (14 miles) southeast of Marsala employs many Tunisian workers. The Old Town is rather like a *kasbah* – white and plain, with just a few solitary palm trees towering over it. The *Piazza della Repubblica* is a beacon in the Baroque design of squares; the interior of the *cathedral* an example of the exceptional quality of Sicilian stucco craftsmanship to be able to imitate every conceivable material using plaster, gold leaf and paint. Maritime archeological finds are displayed in the *Museo del Satiro (daily 9am–7pm | Piazza Plebiscito | admission 6 euros)* in the former church of Sant'Egidio. The highlight is the INSIDER TIP dancing Satyr, a 2 m (6'7") high bronze statue from the 4th century BC. The *Mahara Hotel (81 rooms | tel. 09 23 67 38 00 | www.maharahotel.it | Moderate)* overlooks the palm trees along the sea-front promenade. Mussel lovers head for the *Trattoria delle Cozze Basiricò (on the coast road to Torre Granitola | tel. 09 23 94 23 23 | www.trattoriadellecozze.it | Budget)*.

ROCCHE DI CUSA ● (137 D5) *(ﾛ C5)*

Column drums and capitals intended for the construction of the gigantic Temple G in Selinunte, which were never used, have been lying in the ancient quarry Rocche di Cusa on the edge of Campobello di Mazara for 2500 years. The 1 km/0.6 mile long and narrow archeological area is a picturesque natural site with almond trees. *Combination ticket with Selinunte*

SANTA MARGHERITA DI BELICE (137 E4) *(ﾛ D5)*

The family of the writer Giuseppe Tomasi di Lampedusa owned the large palace *Filangeri Cutò* in Santa Margherita di Belice which, after being destroyed by an earthquake in 1968, was rebuilt on the same site. It is now the Town Hall and literature museum *Museo del Gattopardo (Thu–Tue 9am–1pm, 3pm–6.30pm, Sun only morning | admission 5, guided tour 7 euros | www.parcogattopardo.it/en)*, containing wax figures, books, manuscripts and photographs. Films are also screened here.

SELINUNTE ★ (137 D5) *(ﾛ D5)*

The Greek temples on an elevated plateau above the sea can be seen from a long way away. The columns of two temples have been reconstructed; the others are huge piles of stones. The largest part of this ancient city, 52 km (32 miles) southeast of Marsala, still lies hidden in the earth. The distances within the excavation zone alone and the size of the *Acropolis (daily 9am–sunset | admission 6 euros)* give some idea as to the dimensions of this city, whose heyday resulted from the wheat trade and lasted just 300 years. The modern coastal resort of *Marinella* has extensive sandy beaches, especially around the mouth of the River Belice. *Alceste (26 rooms | tel. 0 92 44 61 84 | www.hotelalceste.it | Moderate)* is a pleasant tourist hotel. The restaurant *Africa (closed Thu | Via Alceste 24 | tel. 0 92 44 64 56 | Moderate)* on the promenade is praised for its wide range of pizzas.

SCIACCA

(137 E5) *(ﾛ D5)* This avalanche of buildings of Sciacca (pop. 41,000) that tumbles down the hill to the fishing harbour looks like an oriental *kasbah*.

The Old Town is a labyrinth only accessible on foot; many streets are just wide enough for two people to pass. The steps to the upper parts of the town date largely from the Arab period. The Old Town is surrounded by a wall with lovely Baroque towers. The main thoroughfare, the *Corso Vittorio Emanuele*, that runs above the steep slope down to the harbour, is lined by palatial residences and the principal churches. Locals meet for their evening *corso* on the large square in front of the Jesuite college. After passing the delightful Baroque *cathedral* you reach the *municipal park* and the *thermal baths*, very much in the turn-of-the-century style when the hot springs and steam fumaroles of Sciacca made it one of the major spa resorts in Europe.

In the 20th-century, Filippo Bentivegna created a bizarre, Baroque-like collection of sculptures with exaggerated features. Row upon row of sculpted stone heads can now be seen in his olive grove. He bequeathed his INSIDER TIP *Castello Incantato (Tue–Sun 9am–1pm and 4pm–8pm (3–5pm in the winter) | admission 5 euros)* to the town of Sciacca.

FOOD & DRINK

HOSTARIA DEL VICOLO
In the upper part of the Old Town, this restaurant serves sardine soup, spaghetti with mint and tuna fish roe, scabbard fish *(spatola)* with olives and capers as well as Baroque-style monastery desserts. *Closed Mon | Vicolo Sammaritano 10 | tel. 0 92 52 30 71 | www.hostariadelvicolo.it | Moderate*

OSTERIA IL GRAPPOLO
Salvatore Ciaccio prepares regional delicacies such as broad bean purée or breaded scabbardfish. Products from the family.owned farm complete the menu. *Closed Tue | Via Conzo 9A | tel. 0 92 58 52 94 | www.osteriailgrappolo.it | Budget– Moderate*

BEACHES & SPORTS

Sandy bays that have not yet been spoilt by mass tourism can be found along the road to Agrigento: INSIDER TIP *Torre Macauda, Torre Verdura* and *Secca Grande* as well as the large nature reserve at the mouth of the Fiume Platani, that stretches as far as *Capo Bianco* below Eraclea Minoa. Secca Grande is a must for divers.

WHERE TO STAY

VILLA PALOCLA
8 rooms with period furniture in a 17th-century country house with its own restaurant, pool and garden. *3 km (1¾ mile) northwest | tel. 09 25 90 28 12 | www.villapalocla.it | Moderate*

INFORMATION

Via Vittorio Emanuele 87 | tel. 0 92 52 04 78

WHERE TO GO

CALTABELLOTTA ☆☆ (137 F5) (*Ø E5*)
Many places in Sicily have been built in daring locations but few are like Caltabellotta (19 km/12 miles northeast of Sciacca), below a range of cliffs with castles and churches growing out of the rock. Authentic recipes such as wild asparagus *frittata,* suckling pig with mint or sweet *cannoli* are served in the authentic and rustic trattoria ⊙ INSIDER TIP *M.A.T.E.S. (Closed Sun evenings | Vicolo Storto 3 | tel. 09 25 95 23 27 | www.matesonline.it | Budget– Moderate)*, reminding guests of the traditional Jewish olive oil trade.

ERACLEA MINOA ★ ☆☆
(137 F6) (*Ø E6*)
The snow-white chalk cliffs 33 km (20½ miles) southeast of Sciacca drop 80 m/262 ft vertically into the sea. Above, on the flat,

are the remains of the ancient town. The *amphitheatre (daily 8.30/9am–sunset | admission 4 euros)*, carved out of the soft stone, is now protected from further erosion under a Plexiglass roof. In nearby Montallegro, INSIDER TIP *Relais Briuccia (8 rooms | Via Trieste 1 | mobile tel. 33 97 59 21 76 | www.capitolo-primo.it | Moderate)* is housed in a restored former nobleman's palace. The rooms are appropriately furnished with 4-posters. At the restaurant, *Capitolo Primo (closed Mon | Moderate– Expensive)*, Damiano Ferraro shows what he has learned at European top restaurants.

white piles of salt; the Egadi islands can be seen out at sea.

The Baroque Old Town, which has survived the air raids of 1943, is hidden behind the elongated harbour. The Renaissance *Palazzo Riccio* has a courtyard with arcades and loggias. The *Palazzo Cavarretto* with the Sicilian eagle gracing its façade forms the end, optically, of the *Corso Vittorio Emanuele*. The magnificent ornamentation on the Jesuite church *Chiesa del Collegio* is typical of the order. The salt-pans outside the town are still partly in operation today. The remaining

Sicily's most daring location: massive rocks tower over Caltabellotta

TRAPANI

MAP INSIDE BACK COVER
(136 C3) *(ΩΩ C3)* **The town (pop. 69,000) sticks out into the sea like a long finger, with 750 m (2460 ft)-high Mount Erice towering up behind. To the south is an endless flat expanse with salt-pans with windmills and dazzlingly**

salt marsh with more than 60 windmills is a listed site.

SIGHTSEEING

MUSEO REGIONALE PEPOLI
This museum is housed in the former convent *Santuario dell'Annunziata* and boasts works by Antonello Gagini and a painting by Titian, among others. Gold work,

coral carvings and majolica pieces are testimonies to the skill of master craftsmen from Trapani. *Tue 9am–1.30pm, Wed–Sat 9am–5.30pm, Sun 9am–12.30pm | admission 6 euros*

FOOD & DRINK

CANTINA SICILIANA
This lively restaurant serving seafood with sea urchin, tuna and squid, is close to the harbour. *Via Giudecca 36 | tel. 09 23 28 86 73 | www.cantinasiciliana.it |* *Moderate*

SAVERINO
On Via Lungomare in *Tonnara di Bonagia* (8 km/5 miles towards San Vito), tasteful design, food prepared by mother and daughters. Also has 20 rooms. *Tel. 09 23 59 27 27 | www.saverino.it | Moderate*

SHOPPING

CORALLI E PREZIOSI
Giusi Damiano and Alfonso Graffeo, two young goldsmiths, bring new life to Trapani's coral tradition. You can watch them create their internationally acclaimed items of jewellery in their workshop. *Via A. Roasi 11 | www.coral liepreziosi.it*

WHERE TO STAY

AI LUMI
Charming B&B in a Baroque palace. Breakfast is served with homemade pastries. *3 rooms | Corso Vittorio Emanuele 74–75 | tel. 09 23 54 09 22 | www.ailumi.it | Moderate*

BAGLIO FONTANASALSA
18th century estate surrounded by olive groves with pool and cookery classes. *9 rooms | on the road to Marsala | tel. 09 23 59 10 01 | www.fontanasalsa.it | Moderate*

INFORMATION

Servizio Turistico Regionale (Piazza Umberto I 15 | tel. 09 23 54 09 93)

WHERE TO GO

AEGADIAN ISLANDS (ISOLE EGADI)
(136 A–B3) *(Ⓜ A–B 3–4)*

Ferries and hydrofoils cross to the three islands off Trapani several times a day. The small limestone islands are surrounded by unpolluted waters; the caves and rich unterwater life attract divers in particular.

Favignana (7½ miles², 33 km/21 miles coastline, pop. 4300) is still one of the most important tuna fisheries today. Soft volcanic tuff was once quarried along the mostly flat rocky coastline and used in the building trade. The bizarre shapes of these quarries right on the shore can still be seen. Most of the island is flat and covered with fields with the 314 m (1030 ft) high *Monte Santa Caterina* rising in the middle with a fortress on the top. Bays suitable for swimming and a few sandy patches can be found in the south of the island. For accommodation and the best seafood try INSIDER TIP *Egadi (11 rooms | Via Colombo 17 | tel. 09 23 92 12 32 | www. albergoegadi.it | Moderate–Expensive).*

Levanzo (2⅓ miles², 12 km/7½ miles coastline, pop. 200) is a 278 m (910 ft) high rocky outcrop which, apart from the fields on the flat part of the island and the terraces above the harbour, is covered by thick *macchia*. The coastline is rugged and rocky. The *Grotta del Genovese (departure from the harbour daily 10.30am and 10.45am | duration of journey/guided tour 2 hrs. | 22.50 euros incl. admission | bookings under tel. 09 23 92 40 32 | mobile tel. 33 97 41 88 00 | www.grottadelgenovese.it)* is a prehistoric cult site. The drawings of animals

Azzurro! Many of the beautiful bays on Favignana can only be reached by boat

carved into the rock are approx. 12,000 years old. The wall paintings of people dancing, animals and idols are some 5000 years old. The cave can be reached by boat or a 4×4. Simple accommodation and good fisherman's fare is available in *Paradiso (23 rooms | Via Lungomare 8 | tel. 09 23 92 40 80 | www. albergoparadiso.eu | Moderate)*.

INSIDER TIP *Marettimo* (4⅔ miles², 19 km/ 12 miles coastline, pop. 700) has a cragged mountain ridge rising 686 m (2250 ft) out of the sea. There are only a few places where the sea can be accessed easily from the land and the marvellous bays and caves are best reached by boat (tours from the harbour). Underwater, Marettimo is a dreamworld. Hikers can follow goat paths up the eastern flank of the island to the ruined fortress *Punta Troia* and to the lighthouse on the even more remote west coast. The Trattoria *Il Pirata (tel. 09 23 92 30 27 | Moderate)* is the island's meeting place, their specialty is pasta with lobster. Accommodation is availabe in private homes – owners are at the harbour to meet the boats.

ERICE ★ ⚓ (136 C3) (𝄞 C3)

14 k m (9 miles) northeast of Trapani, virtually directly above the sea at a height of 700 m/2300 ft, is the medieval town of Erice with its grey stone houses. It is often hidden in the clouds even when the sun is blazing down on the rest of western Sicily. The Elymians and Phoenicians from Asia Minor worshipped Astarte, the goddess of love, and the Romans built a large sanctuary to Venus on the site of the present-day *Norman castle*. Although

the town seems largely deserted, it doesn't show the otherwise so obvious signs of decay as it is the place many Sicilians come to at the weekend to enjoy the cooler air. The view over the plains and salt-pans, the islands in the shallow sea off Marsala, the Aegadian Islands and the rocky coastline of San Vito is quite exceptional. The quickest way to reach this mountian eyrie is by cable car *(June–Aug Mon 1pm–1am, Tue–Fri 7.45am–1am, Sat/Sun 8.45am–2am, Oct–Easter Mon 1pm–8pm, Tue–Sat 8.10am–8pm, Sun 10am–8pm | single ticket 5.50, return 9 euros | www.funiviaerice.it)*.

The stylish *Hotel Elimo (21 rooms | tel. 09 23 86 93 77 | www.hotelelimo.it | Expensive)* and *Hotel Moderno (40 rooms | tel. 09 23 86 93 00 | www.hotelmodernoerice.it | Budget–Moderate)* are in beautiful old town *palazzi*. Try Sicilian top wines at *Monte San Giuliano (closed Mon | tel. 09 23 86 95 95 | www.montesangiuliano.it | Moderate)* which also serves the famous *cuscus alla trapanese*. Information: *Servizio Turistico Regionale (Piazza della Loggia | tel. 09 23 86 93 88)*

SAN VITO LO CAPO (137 D2) *(🗺 C3)*

The 40 km (25 mile) journey along the jagged coastline is magnificent. Bare rock in *Scurati* with inhabited farmhouses next to deserted houses built in a huge cave. Further inland, the *macchia* becomes more dense, broken up by small fields. This is where a trail around the 659 m (2162 ft) high *Monte Cofano* starts, a completely barren rocky mass, a nature reserve that cannot be missed. The circular tour takes approx. 3–4 hours, including a break along the craggy coastline to go for a swim with wonderful views of the shore, the islands and the Zingaro mountain range.

San Vito that lies in a shallow sandy bay close to the promontory with the lighthouse, has grown up around a mighty Saracen tower that has since been converted into a church. The exposed site, the sandy beach and the bizarre cliff formations of *Torre dell'Impiso* have made this into a popular tourist resort.

Hotel Egitarso (22 rooms | tel. 09 23 97 21 11 | www.hotelegitarso.it | Moderate) is right on the shore and has a view of the lighthouse, as has the B & B *Ai Dammusi (3 rooms | tel. 09 23 62 14 94 | www.aidammusisanvito.it | Budget–Moderate)*, an oriental cube with a veranda directly on the sandy beach.

San Vito is well known for its couscous with fish and seafood and a couscous festival is held every year in September. In the other 50 weeks of the year, you can find this speciality at *Alfredo (Contrada Valanga 3 | tel. 09 23 97 23 66 | Moderate)* on the outskirts of the town where the spaghetti with fresh prawns can also be recommended, and in **INSIDER TIP** *Pocho (12 rooms, 3 flats | tel. 09 23 97 25 25 | www.pocho.it | Moderate)* in Makari, 5 km (3 miles) to the south, where the philosopher Marilù Terrasi runs the small hotel with an interesting cuisine and organises musical and theatrical events.

SCOPELLO (137 D2) *(🗺 D3)*

Scopello, 35 km (22 miles) from Trapani, is little more than a fortified farming hamlet located above the cliffs and surrounded by a wall with barren *macchia* beyond. The sea thrashes onto tiny pebbly bays below that are dominated by the *faraglioni* – the high rugged cliffs.

To the north is the boundary of *Zingaro* nature reserve. The old shepherds' cottages are now lived in by local craftsmen or are small country guesthouses, some serving traditional home fare: *La Tavernetta (7 rooms | tel. 09 24 54 11 29 | www.albergolatavernetta.it | Moderate)* and the converted farmhouse set in a garden next door (their own olive oil!), *Casa*

Vito Mazzara (tel. 09 24 54 11 35 | Budget), with five rooms and ten flats. You can book a wonderful farm holiday run by *Camillo Finazzo (11 rooms/flats | tel. 0 92 43 80 51 | www.agriturismofinazzo.com | Budget)* on a mountain in ☙ *Castello di Baida* with a superb view of the coast.

A road leads to the INSIDERTIP *Riserva dello Zingaro* (137 D2) (*Ⓜ C–D3*), although the actual nature reserve can only be accessed on foot. Don't forget your swimming things as there are any number of little paths down to romantic bays. Fan palms grow in this area in the thousands. Although they are generally low-growing bushes, here they can reach a height of 4–5 m (13–16 ft). You are not allowed to leave the well-tended paths, dogs are not allowed. A 7 km (4½ mile) long path along the coast is signposted and easy walking, but remember to take lots of water, something to eat and sunscreen. *(Information at both entrances, in Scopello and Torre dell' Uzzo | daily 7am–7.30pm | admission incl. hiking map 5 euros | www.riservazingaro.it)*. Plan approx. 4 hours for the coastal path, there and back; for the circular path half way up and then back along the coast you'll need 5–6 hours.

Ristorante del Golfo (closed Tue | Via Segesta 153 | tel. 0 92 43 02 57 | www.ristorantedelgolfo.it | Moderate) in the centre of Castellammare serves sea urchin spaghetti and imaginatively prepared fresh seafood. ☙ Hotel *Al Madarig (38 rooms | Piazza Petrolo 7 | tel. 0 92 43 35 33 | www.almadarig.com | Moderate)* is situated above Castellammare's Old Town with a view of Zingaro's coastline.

SEGESTA ★ ☙ (137 D3) (*Ⓜ D4*)

41 km (25½ miles) southeast of Trapani, in a solitary location in the mountains, are the remains of the amphitheatre and temple of an Elymian town, whose residents had adopted the Greek culture and lifestyle, that has long since disappeared. The 5th-century *temple* was never actually completed. The *amphitheatre* further up opens up to the distant sea and the valley below Alcamo. *Daily 9am–7pm (March–Oct until 6pm, Nov–Feb until 5pm) | admission 9 euros*

On the *Fiume Caldo* below Segesta there are thermal springs with a high sulphur content that surface at the end of a deep gorge. On the Castellammare road take the turning to ● *Terme Segestane (thermally-heated swimming pool Fri–Wed 10am–1pm and 4.30pm–midnight (closed Mon mornings) | admission 9 euros)* after the bridge over the river.

The impressive Doric temple in Segesta

THE AEOLIAN ISLANDS

From a long way away, the seven Aeolian islands look like silvery-grey cones hovering above the water. As you draw closer, their volcanic origin becomes perfectly obvious.

The Aeolian (or Lipari) Islands are part of the archipelago around Europe's largest active volcano, the mighty undersea Marsili. Crashing waves have gnawed at the soft tuff and blocks of harder lava can be found along the shoreline which virtually everywhere drops steeply into the sea. Caves, grottoes and arches, small rocky islets and tiny coves and beaches make up a coastline that still remains unspoilt to this day. The colours of the earth and rock are visible through the *macchia* bushes, reeds and tufts of grass, ranging from blinding-white pumice to earthy shades and brilliant reds, greens and jet black lava.

The islands were first settled 6000 years ago. Lipari has the largest deposits of obsidian, the shiny black volcanic glass that was used to make sharp blades, arrowheads, representative daggers and axes up until the Bronze Age. Obsidian from Lipari was exported as far north as Scandinavia, southern Russia and Egypt. Around 1270 BC, the rich deposits drew conquerors from the mainland and it was their king, Liparos, who gave the islands their name. The locals, however, called them "Isole Eolie", after Aeolus, the ruler of the winds in Greek mythology who dwelt in this corner of the Mediterranean and lashed the islands – as he continues to do today. It is not

A magical volcanic kingdom: explore a world of caves and small grottoes, cliffs, hot springs and tiny coves

seldom that storms cut the islands off from the rest of the world for days on end.

Lipari, in particular, is a paradise for hikers, Vulcano for hot water fans, Salina is the caper island with wonderful wines, Panarea is where celebreties and their entourage meet, Stromboli's attraction is its fiery volcano, Filicudi and Alicudi are lonely places with intact nature above and below the water. The islands have been a Unesco World Heritage Site since 1999.

Ferries, hydrofoils *(aliscafi)* and catamarans operate between Milazzo and Lipari, the central point for reaching all of the other islands, several times a day.

"La cucina eoliana", the islanders' fare, was the art of an extremely poor people scraping a living from farming and fishing who nevertheless wanted to gain some enjoyment from their food. Even today, the food they cook makes careful use of what the sea and the gardens provide. The sun, the salty wind off the sea and the minerals in the volcanic earth give tomatoes, aubergines, courgettes and greens an especially intensive aroma. This is accentuated by wild fennel, oregano and capers that no dish goes without and which grow in abundance in every corner of the islands, even in the most barren. In June, you can **INSIDER TIP** pick your own capers along with the islanders. The bushes with their lovely flowers grow all over the place on rocks and walls, particularly on Salina.

the Marina Corta with its little chapel island in front and the bars and restaurants around the *piazza*, narrow alleyways lead up to the citadel and into the Old Town. These are followed by the new straight network of roads with houses and gardens, the majority of the hotels and the main thoroughfare, the *Via Vittorio Emanuele*.

The town is surrounded by hills with terraced fields created at considerable effort,

Tangled nets and hard work: Fishermen on the quayside in Lipari

The buds are mixed with unrefined sea salt which removes the bitter taste and conserves them.

LIPARI

(140 C2) *(∅ K2)* **The town Lipari (pop. 4500) with its Baroque façades and capped church towers is dwarfed by the massive rock of the acropolis (citadel) with its fortress built in the Middle Ages.** The houses nestle around the two bays, the *Marina Lunga* where the ferries come in, and the lively *Marina Corta*. Behind

which – both here and on the other side of the island – are gradually being abandoned. The farmhouses are white cubes with flat domed roofs which collect rainwater for the cisterns and are used for drying grain, figs and nuts in the summer. The fronts have verandas supported by round pillars made of lava or concrete with a reed roof or a pergola.

SIGHTSEEING

ACROPOLIS ☼
The appearance of the citadel, the upper town with churches and noblemen's hous-

es, dates from the Baroque period. Located above the rugged cliffs, this knoll had previously been used by the locals as a place of refuge. The solid medieval town wall had just one gate leading to the Old Town. Reconstructed early tombs and defensive walls can be seen between the churches.

NATIONAL MUSEUM ★

In Antiquity and early history, the Aeolian Islands were a central point for trading throughout the Mediterranean. Rich finds from this time are exhibited in the palaces on the acropolis. One of the highlights is a unique collection of Hellenic theatrical masks made of terracotta. There is also a department on volcanology. *Mon–Sat 9am–7.30pm, Sun 9am–1.30pm | admission 6 euros*

FOOD & DRINK

GILBERTO E VERA

Traditional island establishment at the Marina Corta serving the freshest panini; house wines and an enormous selection of bottles from all over Italy. *Daily in the summer | Via Garibaldi 22 | tel. 09 09 81 27 56 | www.gilbertoevera.it | Budget*

KASBAH ●

Casual lifestyle-choice meeting point with olive garden and reinterpreted down-home country cooking. Lamb with tomato foam or kamut pasta with artichokes. Lipari's best pizza. *Daily in the summer | Vico Selinunte 43 | tel. 09 09 81 10 75 | www.kasbahlipari.it | Budget–Expensive*

INSIDER TIP NENZYNA

Fish trattoria near the small port. The best seats are in the alleyway. *Daily (sometimes closed at lunchtime) | Via Roma 4 | tel. 09 09 81 16 60 | www.ristorantenenzyna.it | Moderate–Expensive*

SHOPPING

Via Vittorio Emanuele is both the place to go for a stroll and to shop. Pretty clothing, capers and some nice bits and bobs can be picked up here.

GIOVANNI SPADA

Do you prefer Aphrodite or Hermes? Terracotta replicas of all Greek Gods and theatre masks ranging from the promiscuous hetaerae to the miser are sold here. Unique Mediterranean souvenirs! *Via Vittorio Emanuele 199*

BEACHES & SPORTS

Boats to the neighbouring islands, beaches and bays depart from the Marina Corta. *Da Massimo (Via Maurolico 2 | tel. 09 09 81 30 86 | www.damassimo.it)* offers boat tours and has rubber boats for hire. *Amici delle Eolie (Corso Vittorio Emanuele 103 | mobile tel. 33 81 58 41 28 | www.amicidelleeolie.it)* offers fishing trips.

★ **National Museum**
A history and geology tour in Lipari → p. 89

★ **Stromboli**
Spectacular: the island's 924 m/3031 ft-high active volcano → p. 92

★ **Punta Milazzese**
A prehistoric village perches on the southernmost point of Panarea → p. 94

★ **Vulcano**
A smoking crater and a wallow in sulphur-smelling hot water → p. 95

MARCO POLO HIGHLIGHTS

Looking over prickly pear cacti and gorse from Lipari to Vulcano

Small cars, scooters and boats can be rented from *Roberto Foti (Via F. Crispi 30 | tel. 09 09 811 370 | www.robertofoti.it)*. Snorkellers should contact the diving school *La Gorgonia (Salita San Giuseppe | tel. 09 09 8126 16 | www.lagorgoniadiving.it)*

ENTERTAINMENT

MARINA CORTA

The area next to the former Aliscafi terminal is basically a huge open-air bar where the locals in particular meet.

WHERE TO STAY

CASA GIALLA

Spend your holidays on an *agriturismo* tomato and vegetable farm in *Pianoconte* with terraces and verandahs outside the 8 rooms. *Mobile tel. 33 94 74 09 02 | www.casagialla.it | Budget– Moderate*

ORIENTE

The 100-year-old villa stands in a garden with a sun terrace not far from the centre. *32 rooms | Via G. Marconi 35 | tel. 09 09 811493 | www.hotelorientelipari. com | Moderate*

INSIDER TIP VILLA ANGELINA

Family-friendly B&B with barbecue area run by a passionate chef. *2 rooms | Via S. Croce | Pianoconte | tel. 09 09 82 22 44 | Budget*

INFORMATION

Information for all the islands available from *Servizio Turistico Regionale (Via Vittorio Emanuele 202 | tel. 09 09 88 00 95)* For more information, see the links under *www.eoliearcipelago.it*

WHERE TO GO

TOUR OF THE ISLAND (140 C2) (*Ø K2*)
The island can be explored by taking the 33 km (20 miles) circular tour with the local taxi *Mirko e Bartolo (mobile tel. 3 68 67 54 00 and 33 81 96 63 78)*. The only beaches accessible by land are on the east coast; the west is much more rugged.

Canneto is a long-drawn out fishing village with a rubble beach. The old lava flow, the Forgia Vecchia – where obsidian was once mined – rises up steeply immediately behind. A footpath in front of the now disused pumice quarry leads to *Spiaggia Bianca*, Lipari's most popular beach. Beyond Acquacalda, the road climbs up to the plateau and the farming communities of ✲ *Quattropani* and *Pianoconte*, which are well worth seeing and from where *Monte Sant'Angelo* (594 m/1950 ft) and the abandoned spa *Terme di San Calogero* can be reached. From the ✲ *belvedere* you have a wonderful view of the neighbouring island, Vulcano. For those on foot, there are tracks and paths down to Lipari past the village *San Bartolo al Monte*, whose pretty church stands at the beginning of the path. A steep footpath into *Valle Muria* branchs off this and leads to a narrow pebbly beach *Spiaggia Muria,* where fishing huts have been built into the rock face. A waymarked ✲ path to the observatory and the southern-most point of the island starts at the church of San Bartolo, and then climbs up high above the east coast and back to Lipari.

SALINA

(140 B–C2) (*$\mathcal{M}$ J2*) **The three islands to the west are away from the general stream of tourists. Salina is also known as the "green island" due to is its extensive farming, chiefly producing Malvasia, a sweet white wine, and capers.**

FOOD & DRINK

A' CANNATA
At the beach in *Lingua*, whose lighthouse marks the southeastern point of the island, seafood is served on long tables in the *pineta*. Also has 8 simple rooms and 9 flats in Lingua. *Daily | tel. 09 09 84 31 61 | www.acannata.it | Moderate*

BEACHES & SPORTS

FOSSA DELLE FELCI ✲
(140 B–C2) (*$\mathcal{M}$ J2*)
The easily recognisable trail starts at the harbour *Santa Marina Salina* and zig-zags up the extinct volcano to 962 m (3156 ft), the highest peak in the Aeolian Islands with an extensive panorama. From here, you can go down to Leni and Rinella. It was in INSIDER TIP *Pollara*, which consists of just a few cuboid houses, and in the fishermen's dwellings carved out of the caves on the tiny beach, that Michael Radford directed the award-winning film "Il Postino" (The Postman), starring Philippe Noiret as Pablo Neruda, in 1994. Pebbly beaches to the east, otherwise a rocky coastline with cliffs that is only accessible from land in a few places *(near Malfa, Pollara* and *Rinella)*.

WHERE TO STAY

HOTEL ARIANA
Art Nouveau villa in *Rinella* on the south coast, with a terrace above the sea. Restau-

LOW BUDGET

The *Baia Unci campsite (Via Marina Garibaldi | tel. 09 09 8119 09 | www.campingbaiaunci.it)* on Canneto beach on Lipari has 8 reasonably-priced bungalows and 10 flats as well as spaces for tents.

Camere Diana Brown (12 rooms | tel. 09 09 81 25 84 | mobile tel. 33 86 40 75 72 | www.dianabrown.it): pleasant accommodation in a side lane off the central Corso Vittorio Emanuele in Lipari.

rant. *15 rooms | tel. 09 09 80 90 75 | www. hotelariana.it | Moderate–Expensive*

HOTEL SIGNUM

The large villa in the centre of *Malfa* has been turned into a boutique hotel; good cuisine. *30 rooms | tel. 09 09 84 42 22 | www.hotelsignum.it | Expensive*

WHERE TO GO

The population of Alicudi and Filicudi, the two islands to the west, has sunk more dramatically than on neighbouring islands. Sheep and goat farming, wine production and cereal crops are no longer viable; as tourist destinations they may well be pretty, but their distance from the other islands makes day-trips that much more difficult.

ALICUDI ● (140 A2) *(ɰ H2)*

The island, a perfectly formed volcanic cone rising out of the sea, is an oasis for those looking for utter peace and quiet. There are only 105 people still living here. Accommodation and food is available in private houses or in the one hotel on the island. The houses – the majority of which have been abandoned – have been built in terraced fields along the main route that leads from the harbour up to the peak at a height of 675 m/2215 ft. *Hotel Ericusa (May–Sept | tel. 09 09 88 99 02 | www.alicudihotel.it | Moderate)*, with 21 simple rooms, is just a few yards from the harbour; the restaurant always serves fresh fish. *Approx. 70 min. from Salina by catamaran*

FILICUDI (140 A–B2) *(ɰ J2)*

The island is dry and covered in high grass and reed. A long scree beach starts at the harbour *Filicudi Porto* and extends as far as the cliffs at Capo Graziano, where the walls of a prehistoric settlement of circu-

lar huts can be found on the knoll. A road leads across the plateau past fields and clusters of houses to the main settlement on the island, *Pecorini*, and down to the harbour and beach at Pecorini Mare. The majority of the coastline with its grottoes, cliffs and rocky pinacles can only be accessed by boat.

The restaurant *Villa La Rosa (Via Rosa 24 | Rocca Ciauli | Filicudi Porto | tel. 09 09 88 99 65 | www.villalarosa.it | Moderate)* has three pretty guest rooms, and the food conjured up by Signora Adelaide is among the best on the island. Apart from seafood, she serves rabbit and her own bread. The hotel *La Canna (14 rooms | tel. 09 09 88 99 56 | www.lacannahotel.it | Moderate)* in Rocca Ciauli has a lovely location high above Filicudi Porto. The *Diving Center Delfini (mobile tel. 34 01 48 46 45 | www.ildelfinifilicudi.com)* in Pecorini is run by Nino Terrano. Its highlight: the shell-encrusted ancient amphorae in the *Museo sottomarino. Approx. 35 min. from Salina by catamaran*

STROMBOLI

(141 D1) *(ɰ K–L1)* ★ Set apart to the north of the others, is the island of Stromboli (pop. 400) with its active volcano, over the summit of which there is always a thin plume of smoke.

The few cuboid houses in *Ginostra* in the south form Italy's most isolated settlement. Buildings straggle the only road towards the north. On every hill is a church, the focal point of the three villages on the island – *San Vincenzo, Ficogrande* and *Piscità.*

A paved path through the high reeds, which later turns into an unmade one with a few dangerous spots, starts at the lighthouse and leads up to the summit.

Groups of hikers normally set off in the afternoon to reach the top before sunset to enjoy the nocturnal spectacle of sheaves of embers that are catapulted out of the crater at short intervals. Hikers must be accompanied by a mountain guide and helmets are compulsory. Take torches and a set of new batteries with you and wear warm, windproof clothing! **INSIDER TIP** *Virtual walks* on the Internet: *www.swisse duc.ch/stromboli*

FOOD & DRINK

LA LAMPARA
Open-air pizzeria with a large terrace and a pizza chef from Naples. Also B&B with seven affordable rooms. *Daily | Via Vittorio Emanuele | Ficogrande | tel. 0 90 98 64 09 | Budget*

PUNTA LENA ● ☼
Exquisite, light, regional cuisine; lots of fish dishes, terrace with pergola and marvellous views. *April–Oct daily | Via Marina 8 | tel. 0 90 98 62 04 | Expensive*

BEACHES & SPORTS

A long scree and gravel beach with black sand in places stretches the length of the three villages on the north coast.

MAGMATREK
Cooperative of volcano guides (also English-speaking). *Via Vittorio Emanuele | tel. 09 09 86 57 68 | www.magmatrek.it.* Appropriate clothing available in the sports shop *Totem (Piazza San Vincenzo 4 | tel. 09 09 86 57 52)*, also for hire.

WHERE TO STAY

Accommodation is expensive. Land-ladies with private rooms to rent meet boats when they come in. Basic accommodation costs from 25 euros p.p. in the low season.

FRANCESCO AQUILONE
Small, friendly guesthouse in San Vincenzo, in luxuriant garden with lemon trees, fisherman's fare. *5 rooms | Via Vittorio*

An eerily beautiful spectacle at night: lava pours down the flanks of Stromboli

Emanuele 29 | tel. 0 90 98 60 80 | www.
aquiloneresidence.it | Budget–Moderate

LA SIRENETTA PARK HOTEL
In 1950, Ingrid Bergman and the crew in Roberto Rossellini's film "Stromboli" stayed here, in what was then a very modest inn. Today, the hotel on the beach in Ficogrande has 55 comfortable rooms. April–Oct | tel. 0 90 98 60 25 | www.lasi renetta.it | Expensive

WHERE TO GO

PANAREA (140 C2) (*ω K1*)
Panarea is the smallest and most fashionable of the islands – in summer, celebrities rub shoulders here with those from the worlds of commerce and banking. The island is surrounded by numerous rocky outcrops and islets – the remains of a collapsed volcano. The three villages Ditella, San Pietro with its harbour, and Drauto run into one another, scattered picturesquely up the jet-black rocky slopes. The west coast is inaccessible, whereas a path down the east coast links the hot steaming fumaroles in the north with ★ Punta Milazzese in the south where, on a ledge 20 m/65 ft above the sea, the walls of a prehistoric village of circular huts can be seen. A path leads to the dreamlike bay Cala Junco surrounded by cliffs. The little island offshore and the rocky cove are the perfect place for swimming and snorkelling.

Experience the expertise at creating exquisite dishes with simple ingredients (rabbit with almonds and oranges!) at INSIDER TIP Da Pina (7 rooms | Via San Pietro 3 | tel. 0 90 98 30 32 | www.panareadapina.it |

FOR BOOKWORMS & FILM BUFFS

Inspector Montalbano – is a Sicilian through and through. He loves good honest food and is always chasing women. The cases were largely filmed in Porto Empedocle and Agrigento, where the author Andrea Camilleri grew up.

Fire at Sea (Fuocoammare) – Shot on the Sicilian island of Lampedusa during the European migrant crisis, it sets the boat migrants' dangerous crossing against the everyday lives of the islanders. This powerful film by Gianfranco Rosi was awarded with the Golden Bear at the 2016 Berlinale.

The Leopard – Claudia Cardinale looks as breathtaking today as she did when the film was released over 50 years and the young Alain Delon is still a beau. Besides watching Luchino Visconti's 1963 classic film adaptation of the best-selling novel "Il Gattopardo" by Giuseppe Tomasi di Lampedusa with Burt Lancaster in the main role, you can also take a tour (in English and Italian) around Palermo following in the footsteps of the actors and the shot scenes. Mondays by appointment only: Sicilia Letteraria (tel. 09 16 25 40 11 | www.parcotomasi.it

Stromboli – Italian-American film (1950) directed by Roberto Rossellini and starring Ingrid Bergman. It features documentary-like scenes of the fishermen's life and an actual evacuation after an eruption of the volcano. As most villagers are played by actual people from the island, it paints a realistic picture of how the islanders lived.

Expensive) with its verandah and garden. *Hycesia (March–Oct | 8 rooms | tel. 0 90 98 30 41 | www.hycesia.it | Moderate–Expensive)* with good seafood, is intimate and – for Panarea – reasonably priced. The *Raya (April–Oct | 29 rooms | tel. 0 90 98 30 13 | www.hotelraya.it | Expensive)*, a hotel with terraced gardens, is built in the local venacular. Its simplicity acts like a magnet for the wealthy. With a boutique and open-air disco. *30–35 minutes from Stromboli by catamaran*

VULCANO

(140 C3) (*M K2*) ★ The holiday island of Vulcano (pop. 300) owes its popularity to its two bays *Porto Levante* and *Porto Ponente*, where there are cliffs, sand and hot fumaroles that don't just heat the water in a few select spots, but with the hot-water and mud-bath *Bagno Termale (admission 3 euros, shower 1 euro)* provide a simple spa area.

A waymarked path leads up to the main crater, the *Gran Cratere*. The smell of pungent sulphur may well indicate that the volcano is dormant but it is still very much alive deep down inside and could well erupt again. A ☀ road along an elevated plain with paroramic views leads to the centre of the island, to *Piano*. A tiny road with hairpin bends carries on to ☀ *Gelso lighthouse* right in the south, which has a magnificent view of the north coast of Sicily and the wall-like Nebrodi mountains behind it, with the summit of Mount Etna towering above them.

FOOD & DRINK

MARIA TINDARA
Up on the mountain in Piano, traditional, serving rabbit, lamb and homemade pasta. *Daily | tel. 09 09 85 30 04 | Moderate*

LA FORGIA DA MAURIZIO
Sicily meets Goa: imaginative seafood dishes near the harbour. *Daily | mobile tel. 33 47 66 00 69 | Budget*

WHERE TO STAY

GARDEN VULCANO
This former captain's house has an impressive collection of memorabilia from around the world. Restaurant and pool.

Not pretty but healthy: wallowing in the mud on Vulcano

Hotel guests also benefit from free entrance to the thermal pool in the Terme di Vulcano. *37 rooms | Porto Ponente | tel. 09 09 85 21 06 | www.hotelgardenvulcano.it | Moderate–Expensive*

ROJAS BAHIA
The hotel is surrounded by a wide green space near the beach in Porto Levante. *April–Sept | 28 rooms | tel. 09 09 85 20 80 | www.hotelrojas.com | Moderate–Expensive*

DISCOVERY TOURS

❶ SICILY AT A GLANCE

START: ❶ Palermo
END: ❶ Palermo

Distance:
🔄 1300 km/808 miles

10 days
Driving time
(without stops)
27 hours

COSTS: approx. 500 euros for 2 people for petrol, motorway toll fees, admissions, cable car/jeep ride up Etna
WHAT TO PACK: swimwear, hiking shoes, long trousers (macchia), sunscreen, sunglasses

IMPORTANT TIPS: book a guide for Mount Etna in advance → p. 38
㉒ Cantina Barone Villagrande: pre-book wine tasting

Would you like to explore the places that are unique to this region? Then the Discovery Tours are just the thing for you – they include terrific tips for stops worth making, breathtaking places to visit, selected restaurants and fun activities. It's even easier with the Touring App: download the tour with map and route to your smartphone using the QR Code on pages 2/3 or from the website address in the footer below – and you'll never get lost again even when you're offline.

TOURING APP

→ p. 2/3

The dazzling diversity of this volcanic island condensed into a ten-day tour: Norman cathedrals, Greek temples, Baroque architecture. Lush vegetation and varied landscapes from the flat vineyards of Marsala to the Riviera dei Limoni craggy coastline, from the smoking hulk of Etna to the limestone Madonie Mountains. Bathers can enjoy beautiful sandy beaches and rocky bays. Culinary delights also await travellers along the route and overnight stays in Syracuse and Taormina promise exciting days with lasting impressions.

Start off from the Sicilian capital ❶ **Palermo** → p. 64 with its magnificent churches, city palaces and lively

DAY 1
❶ Palermo
8 km/5 mi

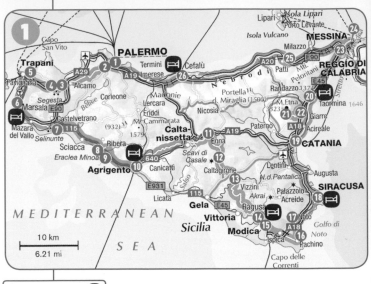

❷ Monreale 🏠	
57 km/35 mi	
❸ Segesta 🏛	
7 km/4.3 mi	
❹ Agriturismo Pocoroba 🍴	
50 km/31 mi	
❺ Erice ☸	
40 km/25 mi	
❻ Marsala 👥 🖼	
DAY 2	
53 km/33 mi	
❼ Selinunte 🏛	
62 km/38 mi	
❽ Riserva Naturale 🌊	
18 km/11 mi	
❾ Eraclea Minoa 🏛	
37 km/23 mi	
❿ Agrigento 🏛 🖼	

markets. Then head for ❷ **Monreale** → p. 71, home to the island's largest Norman cathedral with magnificent mosaics. The colonnaded temple and Greek amphitheatre in ❸ **Segesta** → p. 85 rise up spectacularly along a mountain ridge. ❹ **Agriturismo Pocoroba** *(daily | tel. 33 8113 9150 | www.pocoroba.it | Budget–Moderate)*, **2 km/1.2 mile away in the direction of Bruca,** invites you to an authentic *pranzo*. **The E 933 motorway takes you to Tra-pani** → p. 81, the gateway ferry port to Africa. From here **a steep winding road leads you up to** the scenic mountain top town of ❺ **Erice** → p. 83, 750 m/2461 ft above the plain and the sea. The route continues **past the basins of the salt works** before reaching ❻ **Marsala** → p. 77 where you can sample the local wine in the *bagli,* the historic wine cellars. **Il Profumo del Sale** → p. 77 offers charming accommodation in Marsala.

Take the road **south east via Mazara del Vallo to the coast,** to ❼ **Selinunte** → p. 79, one of the largest Greek cities in Antiquity, today a fascinating archaeological site. **Keep to the coast heading south east.** Stop off at the sandy beach at the mouth of the Platani for a swim in the ❽ **Riserva Naturale** before visiting the Ancient Greek town of ❾ **Er-aclea Minoa** → p. 80 on a snowy white promontory. The next place to head for is ❿ **Agrigento** → p. 72 and the

Valle dei Templi → p. 74, the largest open-air museum of Greek Antiquity on Sicily. Take a tour of the museum in the evening when the temple is lit up magically.

Turn away from the coast and visit ⑪ **Enna → p. 49**, towering above the countryside, that itself is dominated by the fortress **Castello Lombardia** – a pretty spot to enjoy a picnic lunch. ⑫ **Piazza Armerina → p. 50** is reached after passing through an extensively forested area. 5 km/3 miles below, in a verdant river valley, is the INSIDER TIP **Villa del Casale**, a late Roman luxury villa with magnificent floor mosaics that extend over an incredible 4200 m^2/45,000 ft^2 depicting tales of hunting and love. **Continue along the state roads 117 and 124** to the hilltop town of ⑬ **Caltagirone → p. 47**. Here you can marvel at the brightly coloured tiles on the 130 m-long (426 ft) flight of steps and visit ceramicists' studios as well as the **ceramics museum before heading southeast.** Those interested in architecture can explore a highlight of Sicilian Baroque by visiting the twin towns of ⑭ **Ragusa** and **Ibla → p. 53** which are also a magnet for gourmets. Spend the night in the stylish **De Stefano Palace Hotel** *(28 rooms | Via Cav. De Stefano 15 | tel. 09 32 68 28 72 | www.destefanopalacehotel. com | Moderate–Expensive)* and treat yourself in the evening to a prickly pear or carob bean-flavoured ice cream at the **Gelati Divini** on Ibla's cathedral square.

Aztec chocolate to stimulate the senses: **Take the 194 state road** to the fabulous Baroque beauty of ⑮ **Modica → p. 55**, just 20 minutes away, where chocolate makers still produce dairy-free chocolate according to old Spanish Baroque recipes. **From Pacino, head to Sicily's southern-most point** and then return to the sea: In the ⑯ **Vendicari Nature Reserve** near Noto you will find flamingos and wonderful places to swim. The town of ⑰ **Noto → p. 51** is a perfect tribute to urban architecture: it was rebuilt in elegant Baroque style in 1693 after an earthquake. **The route now takes you north** to the port town of ⑱ **Syracuse → p. 55**. It wasn't until the 20th century that this town returned to the size it had reached in Antiquity. Spend two nights here in the boutique hotel **Gutkowski → p. 59** and watch a puppet theatre performed by the **Vaccaro-Mauceri family → p. 119**.

Schedule an entire day to discover Syracuse, the island's capital in the ancient world. Archaeological highlights include the **Greek Theatre**, the gigantic **Ear of Dionysus** dug

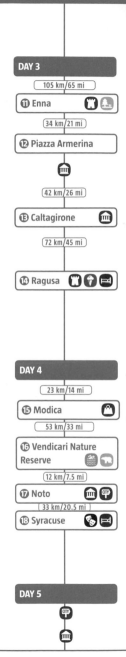

DAY 3

105 km/65 mi

⑪ Enna

34 km/21 mi

⑫ Piazza Armerina

42 km/26 mi

⑬ Caltagirone

72 km/45 mi

⑭ Ragusa

DAY 4

23 km/14 mi

⑮ Modica

53 km/33 mi

⑯ Vendicari Nature Reserve

12 km/7.5 mi

⑰ Noto

33 km/20.5 mi

⑱ Syracuse

DAY 5

out as a rock quarry. Spend the afternoon exploring the Venetian-style old town of **Ortygia** with its many gourmet restaurants or a boat ride to the papyrus sedges along the Ciane River.

After an expresso break at the **Fountain of Arethusa** at the Syracuse port, **take the autostrada north** to the university city of ⑲ **Catania → p. 34**. Join the hustle and bustle of the city's raucous **fish market**, sip an ice-cold almond granita in front of the grand cathedral piazza with its lava stone elephants and check out the boutiques along the Via Etnea. **Now follow the coastal road past the fishing village of Acitrezza and take the slip road at Giarre to ⑳ Taormina → p. 43**, the most popular resort on Sicily. Take in the town's tranquil setting and spend three nights here, for example at the **Villa Schuler → p. 44** owned by a German-Sicilian family since 1905, with a delightful lemon-tree garden and magical breakfast terrace with its view of Mount Etna.

After a relaxing breakfast, stroll along the Corso Umberto to the **Teatro Greco-Romano**, and try the delicious almond marzipan made by the tiny **Pasticceria D'Amore** in the Via Costantino Patricio above the Porta Messina. The afternoon can be spent as you please in one of Taormina's precipitous bays or simply dolce far niente. The family trattoria **Al Giardino → p. 44** welcomes guests with a pleasant and friendly service.

Mount Etna → p. 37 is on today's itinerary. **The road takes you through Giarre and Zafferana Etnea** to the ㉑ **Rifugio Sapienza** at 1910 m/6266 ft. Get out of your car somewhere along the way to take a stroll and acclimatise to the altitude! A cable car or off-road vehicle can take you from the Rifugio further up the volcano. You definitely need a guide (and hiking shoes and rain jacket) if you plan to reach the crater at the top (3340 m/10,958 ft) (which is not always accessible). On the way back down, you can stop at the ㉒ **Cantina Barone Villagrande** *(daily 11am–3.30pm, 6.30pm–10pm and on appointment | Via del Bosco 25 | Milo | tel. 09 57 08 21 75 | www.villagrande.it)*, built in 1727 in beautiful surroundings 3 km/1.9 mile north of Zafferana Etnea, to taste the *Rosso del Etna,* a wine made from autochthonous grapes, served with antipasti. Spend your afternoon pleasantly doing nothing or swimming in Taormina's steep bays.

DAY 6

87 km/54 mi

⑲ Catania

54 km/33 mi

⑳ Taormina

DAY 7

DAY 8

55 km/34 mi

㉑ Rifugio Sapienza

24 km/15 mi

㉒ Cantina Barone Villagrande

Towering high above the lagoon is the revamped pilgrimage church of Tindari

To speed up your journey, take the toll motorways northbound. Drive through the Art Nouveau-style boulevards of 23 Messina → p. 40 and take the splendid route **along the Stretto di Messina strait** as far as 24 Punta Faro, where Sicily and the Calabrian mainland almost meet (3 km/1.9 mile apart). **Then head west to the slip road at Villafranca** and from there on to 25 Tindari → p. 42. Join the pilgrims to the Black Madonna in the pilgrimage church on the Capo Tindari high above the sea with views over to the Aeolian Islands. **Another worthwhile detour along the E 90 motorway** is the picturesque 26 Cefalù → p. 60, the perfect place to spend the night. The historic centre lies at the foot of the 270 m/885 ft high precipitous limestone La Rocca which makes the medieval old town and the Norman cathedral look tiny in comparison.

West of the old town lies a sweeping sandy bay with harbour promenade, the perfect spot for a last dip in the sea **before heading west along the autostrada** back to the capital 1 Palermo → p. 64.

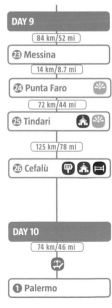

DAY 9

84 km/52 mi

23 Messina

14 km/8.7 mi

24 Punta Faro

72 km/44 mi

25 Tindari

125 km/78 mi

26 Cefalù

DAY 10

74 km/46 mi

1 Palermo

2 ON THE VIA DEL SALE

START: ❶ Trapani END: ❻ Marsala	8 hours Driving time (without stops) 3.5 hours
Distance: ➡ 43 km/27 miles	

COSTS: approx. 60 euros per person for bike hire, couscous meal, admissions, crossing to Mozia
WHAT TO PACK: sunscreen, drinking water

IMPORTANT TIPS: It gets extremely hot in summer. The salt lakes reflect sunlight so don't forget your sunglasses.
Bike hire everywhere in Trapani. From Marsala, trains *(www.trenitalia. it)* that allow bikes on board depart every hour to two hours and return to Trapani in about 30 minutes. Alternative: *Taxi Eugenio (mobile tel. 3 286 038 751)* for approx. 50 euros

Tracking down white gold: The Via del Sale, the Salt Route, runs along minor roads down the coast from Trapani to Marsala. As clear as the boundary between the sea and the land may appear to be where the low-lying limestone meets the water, optically the sky, the salt lakes, the lagoons and the flat islands with their rows of pine trees and deserted houses merge into one creating a melancholic landscape. The cragged rocky peak of Eryx looms up above the plains just as suddenly as the three islands Favignana, Levanzo and Marettimo appear out of the water.

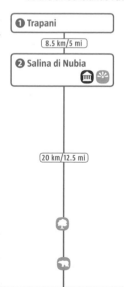

❶ Trapani

8.5 km/5 mi

❷ Salina di Nubia

20 km/12.5 mi

09:00am In ❶ Trapani → p. 81 **take the SP 21 minor road to Marsala** (signposted Airport/Birgi, later Via del Sale). **5 km/3 miles south of Trapani there is a turning to the** ❷ **Salina di Nubia**. Here the Culcasi family shows the different stages of traditional salt production in the **Museo del Sale** *(daily 9.30am–7pm | admission 2 euros | www.museodelsale.it)*. Take in the views of the nearest Aegadian Islands → p. 82 Favignana and Levanzo and to the promontory in the north dominated by Erice → p. 83.

Returning to the strada provinciale 21, follow the directions for Marsala until you reach the turning to Birgi Novo, a village of single-storey houses surrounded by vineyards, beyond the airport. Ride along a narrow lane **heading south along the banks of the lagoon.** Between 30 cm and 4 m (1–13ft) deep, the lagoon has a wealth of underwater flora and is a natural habitat for water birds such as pink flamingos.

12:00pm On a level with the island of Mozia is the largest operating salt works, ❸ INSIDER TIP ▸ **Ettore Infersa** (*daily 9am–8pm | admission free | www.salineettoreinfersa.com*). You can visit the salt lakes, a museum and a windmill and buy some of the white gold in pretty packaging as a unique souvenir. A few steps further is the quay with the ❹ **Trattoria Mamma Caura** (*daily | mobile tel. 38 88 77 24 99 | www.mammacaura.it | Budget–Moderate*) in the design of the Cyclades where you can try the regional speciality *cuscus con pesce* in fish stock served with a dry white Grillo or Cataratto wine. Lock up your bike and catch a small ferry boat over to Mozia (*takes approx. 5 minutes | April–Oct 9.15am–6.30pm, Nov–March 9.15am–2pm | 5 euros | www.mozialine.com*).

The settlement of ❺ ★ **Mozia** (Mothya) on the partly wooded island of **San Pantaleo** was a fortified Phoenician port and important trading hub until its destruction by the Greeks in 397 BC. Archaeological ruins still exist today. A walk around the island with its profusion of pines, palms and vineyards takes approximately one hour. In the south are the basins and walls of the 2500-year old **harbour;** in the north the **urn graveyard** with roughly-hewn gravestones. At the **Cappiddazzu** excavation site there once stood a monumental temple to Tanit, the principal goddess together with Baal of the Carthaginians who turned the island into a strategic base. The villa, once belonging to the English wine magnet Joseph Whitaker, now houses the **museum** (*island visit incl. museum and archaeological zones daily 9am–3pm, April–Oct. 9.30am–6.30pm | admission 9 euros | www.fondazionewhitaker.it*) with finds from the Punic past of Mozia and Marsala. The highlight is a life-sized marble figure, the *Ephebe of Mozia*, probably a Greek-Punic sculpture from the 5th century BC of a young male figure dressed in a transparent robe with a wealth of folds.

❸ Ettore Infersa

350 m/382 yd

❹ Trattoria Mamma Caura

1.5 km/1 mi

❺ Mozia

Snow-covered Etna in stark contrast to the gentle rolling hills around Enna

13 km / 8 mi

6 Marsala

04:00pm Returning to the mainland, **follow the coastal road** – passing through fishing villages, holiday homes and African-style palm-lined alleys leading to vineyard villas – back to **6** Marsala → p. 77. Return to Trapani on the train.

3 WHEAT FIELDS AND SULPHUR MINES

START: **1** Enna END: **10** Castrofilippo	1 day Driving time (without stops) 5 hours
Distance: **→** 245 km/152 miles	

COSTS: approx. 50 euros per person for petrol, admissions, guided tours, donations, evening meal
WHAT TO PACK: protective footwear

IMPORTANT TIPS:
Pre-book guided tours of the **2** railway museum
Information on the Vulcanelli di Macalube at *Riserva Naturale Macalube* (tel. *09 22 69 92 10* | *www.legambienteriserve.it*)

The region around Caltanissetta was the world's largest sulphur mine in the 19th century. Today, the endless ranges of hills and mountains have been returned to crops as it used to be in Antiquity. This route takes you along some of the island's smaller winding roads to some of Sicily's most authentic places. Along the way you may see groups of men in *coppola* flat caps sitting around, discussing in sign language.

`09:00am` **Road 121** leads from **❶ Enna** → p. 49 into the wide valley of the Fiume Salso. The autostrada twists through the countryside here sometimes on bridges that are up to 10 km/6 miles long. In **❷ Villarosa** there are seven, bright-red freight wagons at the station which the former stationmaster Primo David has turned into a `INSIDER TIP` **museum** *(Tue–Sun 9.30am–12.30pm and 4.30pm–7.30pm, by appointment | mobile tel. 33 84 80 97 21 | admission 5 euros | www.trenomuseo villarosa.com)* on the history of the area and the railway, sulphur mining, agriculture and emigration. To date, there are 2500 objects ranging from a whistle to a prince's bedroom, collected from Villarosa, the rest of Sicily and from all over the world.

`01:00pm` **Take the A 19 motorway south** to the former sulphur mining centre **❸ Caltanissetta**. The market stands, street kitchens and narrow alleyways in the old town remind you of an oriental bazaar. Take in a bite to eat here before visiting the gigantic, unfinished Baroque **Palazzo Moncada,** an architectural treasure.

Mussomeli is reached **along the winding, narrow road via San Cataldo.** 2 km/1¼ mile before you get there you will pass **❹ Castello Manfredonico** from the 12th centu-

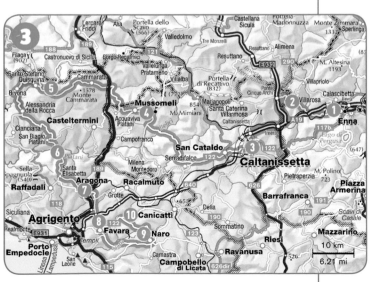

Ornate Baroque altar with the Santa Rosalia di Quisquina

ry located on a rocky promontory that made it unassailable. From the top, you can see most of Sicily on a clear day. **Via Santo Giovanni Gemini and Cammarata** you reach **Monti Sicani**, with its forests and many springs. It is worth making a short detour to the Greek-style ❺ **pilgrimage church of Santa Rosalia di Quisquina (side road on the right 3 km/1½ mile before reaching Santo Stefano Quisquina)** where the patron saint of Palermo lived in a cave as a hermit in the 12th century.

From Santo Stefan di Quisquina, drive through Alessandria della Rocca to ❻ **San Angelo Muxaro,** an Albanian settlement boldly sited on a mountain plateau. Below the town is a waymarked footpath from the road to prehistoric **rock tombs** from the pre-Hellenic period. **Continue south** to refreshingly un-touristy ❼ **Aragona.** Take a break at the favourite bar of locals, **Pasticceria La Preferita** *(Via Roma 217)*, to taste their marzipan dolci and cappuccino which are out of this world and sprinkled with flaked pistachios harvested in the Platani valley nearby! Authentic Sicilian folk art is on display at the **Chiesa Madre** with its INSIDER TIP nativity scene filled with lots of crib figures. The nearby Vulcanelli di Macalube mud craters are expected to remain closed for some time due to an accident.

08:00pm The route now offers various impressions through art history, taking you to the Baroque countryside towns of ❽ **Favara** and ❾ **Naro,** where sculptors and stonemasons let their fantasy run wild and carved faces, masks, grotesque caryatids, pillars, sills and squiggles out of the soft, dark-yellow sandstone to adorn the façades of churches and palaces. Finish your tour with an evening *cena* with stuffed cabbages and quails at **Osteria Cacciatore** *(closed Wed and lunchtime except on Sundays | Via Puglia 5 | tel. 09 22 82 98 24 | Budget)* in nearby ❿ **Castrofilippo,** which is run by five sisters.

---

37 km/23 mi

❺ pilgrimage church of Santa Rosalia di Quisquina 🏠

44 km/27 mi

❻ San Angelo Muxaro 🌳 🏛 🏠

16 km/10 mi

❼ Aragona ☕ 🏠

13 km/8 mi

❽ Favara 🏛 🏠

15 km/9 mi

❾ Naro 🏛 🏠

15 km/9 mi

❿ Castrofilippo 🍴

4

THE GREEN GIANTS

START: ❶ Piano Sempria	3 hours
END: ❶ Piano Sempria	Hiking time
	(without stops)
Distance: easy	1.5 hours
🚶 3.5 km/2.5 mi ▮▮ Altitude: 180 m/591 ft	

COSTS: 25 euros per person for picnic and evening meal
WHAT TO PACK: rain jacket, sunscreen, hiking shoes, drinking water, picnic

IMPORTANT TIPS: you can buy everything you need for a picnic in Castelbuono. Information also available at *www.parcodellemadonie.it*

With a prickly trunk to ward off goats and smooth, spineless leaves at the top, the giant holly trees of Piano Pomo in the Madonie Mountains are the oldest of their kind in Europe. These evergreen hollies grow to 15 m/50 ft in height and have thick foliage. This botanic walk takes you uphill along technically undemanding terrain, passing dramatic scenery and with splendid panoramic views. The Madonie Mountains are the central part of a long limestone chain that rises above Sicily's north coast. Inland, they form an upland plateau that is almost 2000 m/6600 ft high.

Bright red berries and deep green leaves: the giant holly trees are the attraction of Piano Pomo

The start of this mountain hike is ❶ Piano Sempria (1260 m/4134 ft), which you can reach from **Castelbuono → p. 64 along a 10 km/6 miles long mountain road.** An information board at the beginning of the path *(sentiero natura)* shows the route. At the hollow, 800-year-old oak, in which there is a small statue of the Virgin Mary, **the path crosses the road and zig-zags its way up** through the steep oak woodland to a **viewpoint**.

The climb finishes here **and the path continues below a rock face along the slope and runs into a track which passes over a gate** onto the grassy ❷ **Piano Pomo** (1380 m/4528 ft). There is a *pagghiaru (pagliaio)* here – an elongated stone building with a roof of brushwood, with tables and benches inside. It was built for forest workers and hikers along the lines of a Sicilian shepherd's hut and is the perfect place for a relaxed morning picnic.

Climb over the fence using the wooden steps and after a few yards down a path you'll come to a **grove of giant holly trees** *(Aquifoli giganti)*. This plant has its origins in the Ice Age. There are around 100 trees which are estimated to be 300 years old and more. It is quite dark among the thick trunks as little light penetrates the dense foliage which prompts local hiking guides to call it the *"cattedrale della natura"*. Beyond the grove next to an ancient beech tree *(faggio secolare)*, **an easily recognisable path on the right leads** through beech and oak woodland, with equally huge tree trunks, to the cross on the summit of ❸ **Cozzo Luminario** (1512 m/4961 ft), from which you have a panoramic view in all directions taking in the sea, the Aeolian Islands, Etna and the high plateau of Pizzo Carbonara (1979 m/6493 ft).

The path then descends into a dip in the karst rocks of ❹ **Piano Imperiale**, and from there **onto the forest track** that will bring you back to ❶ **Piano Sempria**. Hearty food, such as tagliatelle with mushrooms

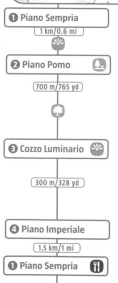

❶ Piano Sempria

1 km/0.6 mi

❷ Piano Pomo

700 m/765 yd

❸ Cozzo Luminario

300 m/328 yd

❹ Piano Imperiale

1.5 km/1 mi

❶ Piano Sempria

and pork from free-range pigs, are to be had at the mountain lodge **Rifugio Francesco Crispi** *(28 beds | tel. 09 21 67 22 79 | www.rifugio-crispi.it | Budget)* run by the Club Alpino Siciliano.

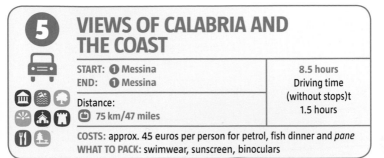

⑤ VIEWS OF CALABRIA AND THE COAST

START: ❶ Messina END: ❶ Messina	8.5 hours Driving time (without stops)t 1.5 hours
Distance: 🚗 75 km/47 miles	

COSTS: approx. 45 euros per person for petrol, fish dinner and *pane*
WHAT TO PACK: swimwear, sunscreen, binoculars

This tour goes from the Caravaggio paintings in Messina to the lagoon pools where clams *(vongole veraci)* and mussels *(cozze)* are farmed – and of course to a fish trattoria. From the northern-most point on the island it goes up to the ridge of the Monti Peloritani with breath-taking views of the strait Stretto di Messina, the coast and the mountains of Calabria, the Aeolian Islands, the Ionian and Tyrrhenian Seas. The geographical peak is the Monte Antennamare (or Dinnamare as Sicilians call it).

`10:00am` Start at the cathedral square in ❶ **Messina** → p. 40 and **follow the coastal road Viale della Libertà north to no. 465.** Enjoy almost a private viewing of two of Caravaggio's master paintings in the picture gallery of the **Museo Regionale** → p. 41, "Adoration of the Shepherds" and "The Raising of Lazarus" (both painted in 1609) are fine examples of the painter's light-dark technique (parking spaces are available on the opposite side of the road). **Back on the Via Libertà, take a left shortly after the museum uphill along the Via della Annunziata and then follow the panoramic SP 43 north until you reach the fishing village of** ❷ **Ganzirri**. What was once a spot for wallowing wild boar is now two lagoon pools *(pantano grande/piccolo)* that are famous for mussel farming. Locals swear by the eel patties and *spaghetti con vongole* served at the **Trattoria del Lago** *(Closed Fri and in the evenings | Via Lago Grande 92 | tel. 0 90 39 22 75 | www.trattoriadellago.it | Moderate)* which has been serving *cucina messine* for more than 50 years.

❶ Messina

11 km/7 mi

❷ Ganzirri

5 km/3.1 mi

5

Capo Rasocolmo

ACQUARONE

SPARTA **5** **4**

SANTA SABA

Casa Bianca

113 dir.

Massa
San Giorgio

Massa San Nicolo

Punta del Faro
o Capo Peloro

MORTELLE

SINDARO
MARINA

Monte Pace
419

Massa
Santa Lucia

FARO
SUPERIORE

320

Pantano
Grande

3 COLONIE

CASTANEA
DELLEFURIE

Massa San Giovanni

415

CURCURACI

2

TORRE FARO

GANZIRRI

SANT' AGATA

422

SALICE

Trivio

GROTTA

Messina

Messina Nord/
Villafranca
Tirrena

A20

609

PACE

P

GESSO

Monte Ciccia

Rizzotti

CONTEMPLAZIONE

PARADISO

Villa

San
Nicolò

P

Urni

SANTISSIMA
ANNUNZIATA

SALVATORE
DEI GRECI

San Giovanni

Piale

(15)

Acciarello

Serro

Calvaruso

Settentrionale
Sicula

524

9 **6** **8**

BADIAZZA

Messina-
Giostra

MESSINA

(3)

E45

E90

113

Concessa

A3

Pizzo Chiarino

CAMARO

841

Messina
Boccetta

Fiera
Sant. di
Montalto

Messina

CATARRATTI

CASALOTTO

Duomo

CATONA

Nunziatella

BORDONARO

Messina Centro

A18

CUMIA

Messina
Gazzi

SANTO

GALLICO MARINA

Dinnammare

San Filippo
Superiore

San Filippo
Inferiore

7

1127

GAZZI

CONTESSE

Zafferia

E45

SANTA
LUCIA

PISTUNINA

Tremestieri

LARDERIA

Tripoldo

Messina Sud-
Tremestieri

TREMESTIERI

P

2 km

1.24 mi

3 Punta del Faro

11 km/6.8 mi

02:00pm After your mussel feast, **head to the coast along
the increasingly narrowing strait to Sicily's most northeast point** called **3** **Punta del Faro**, or Capo Peloro as
it was called in Antiquity. From the beach you can see
the Rock of Scilla on the other side of the strait and the
whirlpools just off the coast that form in the shallows and
along the sandbanks of Cariddi. They pose a danger to
small ships even today. In Homeric mythology they eat
sailors as the sea monsters Scylla and Charybdis. This
is where the 3 km/1.8 mile bridge across the shallow
banks was to be built before the project was cancelled
in 2013 soon after it had been started. From the Punta
del Faro, head west to visit tiny seaside resorts such as

④ Acquarone with numerous bathing areas and craggy coastline interspersed with sandy and pebble beaches to **⑤ Spartà**, Sicily's most northern point. **The road then runs along the ridge of the Peloritani mountains to ⑥ Colle San Rizzo** (624 m/2047 ft) **and along the same road to ⑦ Monte Antennamare**, 1130 m/3707 ft above sea level, where there is a **pilgrimage church** dedicated to the Virgin Mary. The view from up here takes in the Tyrrhenian Sea and Sicily's north, the Aeolian Islands and, to the east, Messina, the strait and Calabria's southern headland. To the south and west you can make out the mountain valleys and peaks of Monti Peloritani. The woods in the vicinity with cool springs and picnic places are the ideal spot for a relaxing break.

06:00pm **Returning to Colle San Rizzo,** it is worth making a detour halfway back to Messina, to **⑧ Badiazza**, the romantic ruins of a fortified church with a tower and battlements from the Norman period. To end the tour, try some local fast food at the authentic **⑨ Kiosk Don Mincio** (www.donmincio.com) **at the crossroads to the Settentrionale Sicula 113:** the spicy pane della disgraziata is highly recommended. Now return to the port of **① Messina** → p. 40 a**long the steep winding road 113.**

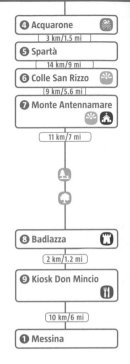

④ Acquarone

3 km/1.5 mi

⑤ Spartà

14 km/9 mi

⑥ Colle San Rizzo

9 km/5.6 mi

⑦ Monte Antennamare

11 km/7 mi

⑧ Badlazza

2 km/1.2 mi

⑨ Kiosk Don Mincio

10 km/6 mi

① Messina

Ciao Italia: view of the Italian mainland from the beach at Punta del Faro

SPORTS & ACTIVITIES

Sicily boasts a coastline of more than 1000 km (620 miles). With the exception of a few short sections around major urban centres, the water is invitingly clean. No fewer than 17 beaches are permitted to fly the prestigious blue flag, *bandiera blu,* for its high water quality standards.

Watersports such as snorkelling and diving, sailing and surfing are possible all round the island. On terra firma, hikers, mountainbikers and horseriders in particular get their money's worth too.

DIVING

Ideal conditions prevail for divers and snorkellers above rocky terrain. This can be found off the north coast in particular or on the east coast around Etna. By far the best diving grounds are around the small islands – first and foremost Ustica as well as Lampedusa off the coast of Africa. The areas around the Aegadian and Aeolian Islands, however, are almost as good.

All islands have a well-established infrastructure for underwater fans (diving courses, equipment for hire, cylinder service, decompression tanks).

Diving around *Ustica* (hydrofoil *aliscafo* from Palermo): the waters are a protected maritime reserve and are considered by Italian divers to be the best of their kind. In summer packed; otherwise sufficient private accommodation available. Information: *Riserva Marina di Ustica (tel. 09 18 44 81 24 | www.ampustica.it)*

Up mountains, in the countryside, under water and in the air: the best places for your favourite sports and activities

GOLF

Although golf is a relatively young sport in Sicily, there are now six golf courses on the island. Situated 10 km/6 miles to the east of Sciacca, the *Verdura Resort (250 rooms and suites | Strada Statale 115/km 131 | tel. 0 95 99 81 80 | www.roccofortehotels.com | Expensive)* not only offers the ultimate golfing experience for serious golfers, it is an all-inclusive and highly exclusive design hotel with infinity pool, tennis courts and

three golf courses. In contrast, hobby-putters can try their hand at the 9-hole club of the *Villa Airoldi (Piazza Leoni 9 | tel. 0 91 54 35 34 | www.villaairoldigolf club.com)*. Other golf addresses: *lea dingcourses.com*.

HIKING

The mountains, wild upland plateaus and impressive gorges, especially those in the southeast, are not often visited by local hikers. Many trails follow the *trazzeri*, the old cattle routes, that are no longer used today. There are few maps marking footpaths for hikers and few signposts. However, in the five large nature reserves – Etna, the River Alcantara, the Nebrodi, Madonie and Monti Sicani chains – you will be able to find your way easily and choose between hikes of varying degrees of difficulty. Hiking through gorges, which often carry water at all times of year, is only suitable for experienced mountaineers. Guided hikes in the nature reserves are generally available at the weekends.

Cava d'Ispica: 10 km (6¼ miles)-long gorge with caves at either end that can be visited. Tours depart from the *Ispica visitor centre* at the entrance to the gorge.

Parco Regionale delle Madonie (Petralia Sottana | Corso Pietro Agliata 16 | tel. 09 21 68 40 11 | www.parcodellemadonie.it)

Parco Regionale dei Nebrodi (Alcara Li Fusi | Via Ugo Foscolo 1 | tel. 09 41 79 39 04 | www.parcodeinebrodi.it)

Parco Regionale dell'Etna (Nicolosi | tel. 0 95 82 11 11 | www.parcoetna.ct.it)

Parco Fluviale dell'Alcantara (Via dei Mulini | Francavilla di Sicilia | tel. 09 42 98 99 | www.parcoalcantara.it)

Parco Regionale dei Monti Sicani (www.parcodeisicani.it)

You can take a visual hike on the web under *www.greenstontrek.com* and *www.artemisianet.it*.

MOUNTAINBIKING

It is possible to cycle virtually all over the island along little-used side roads, tracks across farmland and through forests. Etna, Madonie, Nebrodi and the Peloritani mountains have challenging changes in altitude, often rising above 1000 m (3000 ft). It is less strenuous along the south coast, in the west and on the limestone plains around Syracuse and Ragusa.

A challenging tour leads along the

⚡ INSIDER TIP *ridge of the Peloritani mountains* with views over the northernmost point of Sicily, the strait, the Calabrian mountains and Etna, the Aeolian Islands and the Tyrrhenian and Ionian Seas. The tour starts in *Messina* at the *Portella di Rizzo* (466 m/1529 ft), running along the ridge (1100–1200 m/3600–4000 ft) to *Portella Mandrazzi* (1125 m/3691 ft), then twists through a series of hairpin bends to *Castroreale/Milazzo* or *Taormina* – a total of 95 km (59 miles) from Messina to Taormina. Good, up-to-date information (in English) under *on-sicily.com/cycling-in-sicily*

RIDING

Riding is popular, especially in the Madonie Mountains, often as part of a guided day's ride: *Azienda Agrituristica Monaco di Mezzo (Petralia Sottana | tel. 09 34 67 39 49 | www.monacodimezzo.com)*. More addresses: *www.turismoequestre.com*

SAILING

The sailing tourism industry is less developed here than in the north of Italy. First-class sailing is possible between Tropea (Calabria), the Aeolian Islands and along the north coast from Tindari to Cefalù. Passing through the Strait of Messina, the *Stretto*, is an exciting experience. This is a very demanding stretch of water due to the shallows, changing currents, sudden winds and the traffic. Or sail along the slopes of Etna on the attractive east coast with numerous small fishing ports as far as Catania.

WELLBEING

The island's sulphur springs and healing waters were already known to the

Keeping dry: exploring caves in the Alcantara Gorge the easy way

ancient Hellenes, and Richard Wagner visited Acireale's thermal baths. However the island has only recently woken up to the health and wellness craze, transforming many of its ancient spa resorts into modern facilities and *centri benessere.* Guests can now choose between thermal baths, wellness hotels or family favourites such as the *mud baths* at the harbour in Vulcano (see p. 95).

WINDSURFING

The best places to surf are on the west and south coasts as there is almost always sufficient wind: San Vito Lo Capo, Favignana, Torre Granitola and Triscina near Selinunte, Torre di Gaffe near Licata and Capo Passero in the southeast. Capo Orlando on the north coast is also popular among surfers.

WINTER SPORTS

The two winter sports areas on Sicily are Etna and the Madonie Mountains where, concentrated in a few spots, there are hotels, lifts and ski schools. At weekends when the weather is good, things are very busy especially from January until March when you can be certain of snow. On Mount Etna, above Nicolosi, 1800 m (5900 ft) above sea level, is the main winter sports centre *Etna Sud* which – despite the recent eruptions – has a number of lifts as well as accommodation. In the Madonie Mountains, almost everything is centred on *Piano Battaglia* (1650 m/5410 ft). The tracks high up in the Nebrodi and Madonie mountains are ideal for cross-country skiing. They are partly marked as the long-distance path *Sentiero Italia.*

TRAVEL WITH KIDS

All Italians are wild about children. They would do anything for bambini. And parents are automatically part and parcel of this open demonstration of kindness, whether on a beach, in a hotel or elsewhere.

Sicily has superb holiday adventures in store for children – much more than just sand, sun and ice cream, even if it may not seem the perfect holiday destination for children at first glance. Museums with their endless corridors, excavation sites exposed to the scorching sun, churches, monasteries and palaces on every corner, and the relatively long distances along never-ending twisty roads with no shade: all these things are pretty demanding on children. Apart from the Luna Park with its merry-go-rounds and beaches with bright plastic toys which can be found in most seaside holiday resorts in the summer, there is little for children and even less that comes with the stamp: "educationally beneficial". So get active yourself! And "when in Rome"... do as the Sicilians do! Take advantage of the cool mornings, enjoy a siesta with the children and have a quiet afternoon. In the evening it is a bit cooler and you'll feel fitter again.

In trattorias (though not in first-class restaurants), even five-year-olds are considered "normal" eaters even if they only jab at the food put in front of them. If your child only wants the spaghetti or the fish, just let the waiter know. He'll understand and accept it. Go for picnics like the Sicilians do, especially at the weekends, when things get pretty hectic elsewhere.

Exceptionally family-friendly: boat trips and railways journeys, exploring caves, puppet theatres and as much sea as you could want

There are masses of picnic sites in the wooded mountains, many with spring water fountains which can be used to keep fruit and drinks for the children cool. Flat beaches with fine, soft sand where children can splash around quite safely, dig or build sandcastles, cannot be found all over Sicily. There is a long sandbank south of Syracuse that runs almost 300 km (185 miles), virtually the whole length of the south coast as far as Selinunte, with the exception of a few rocky sections. The softest and finest sand is in *Fontane* *Bianche* near Syracuse and on the *Marina di Noto*; south of Ragusa are the wide beaches and dunes of *Pozzallo, Sampieri, Donnalucata* and *Scoglitti*, near *Falconara* to the west of Gela, in *San Leone* (Agrigento) with a number of beach facilities, around *Siculiana Marina*, in *Eraclea Minoa*, around the mouth of the *Fiume Platani* southeast of Sciacca, *Porto Palo di Menfi* and *Marinella* near Selinunte. In the north and east there are only a few short sections, but the water here can get deep quite suddenly. The best places include

San Vito Lo Capo (town beach), Mondello near Palermo with unpolluted water and flour-like sand, Cefalù (town beach), Capo Orlando, the coast between Tindari and Milazzo, Letoianni, Giardini-Naxos with the extremely child-friendly but often over-crowded beaches of San Marco and Fondachello to the south, and finally the flat plain south of Catania with a number of lidos. The islands around Sicily have very few beaches suitable for children.

THE NORTHEAST

ETNALAND (143 D2) *(ᗰ K5)*

Pinball cinema, cable car ride and dinosaur park – funfair and water park (theme park Acquapark open April–Sept), at steep prices. *Daily 9.30am–6.30pm (entrance until 4pm), July/Aug also 7.30pm–1am | admission 25–38 euros (evenings 20–30 euros), children under 1.40 m in height 20–28 euros (15–20 euros), children under 1 m free | Contrada Agnelleria | Belpasso | near Paternò | www.etnaland.eu*

THE SOUTHEAST

INSIDER TIP ▶ BUSCEMI – REDISCOVERING OLD TRADES (143 D4) *(ᗰ K7)*

This village is a mixture of a museum and a craft workshop. You can walk around authentic farmhouses and a water mill as well as watch basket makers, carpenters and weavers at work. *Museo della Civiltà Contadina (Mon–Fri 8am–1pm, Sat 8am–noon | guided tour (2 hrs.) 5 euros, children up to 6 free, 6–18 years old 3.50 euros | tel. 09 31 87 85 28 | www.museo buscemi.org)*

RAILWAY TRIP

(142–143 B5–E4) *(ᗰ J–K7)*
Between Syracuse and Vittoria, a regular train service climbs up to the high plateau

of Ragusa from sea level and back down to the sea again in a 3-hour journey which is better than any museum line. It twists and turns around massive bends and loops, crosses several deep gorges, sometimes on heart-stoppingly high viaducts. *3 times daily | fare 9.40 euros, children up to 12 years old 4.70 euros | www.trenitalia.com*

AGRIMILO DONKEY BREEDING SANCTUARY ⊕ (143 D5) *(ᗰ K7)*

Onoterapia – what's that, you may ask? Quite simply donkey riding as a type of therapy for parents and great fun for kids. This agriturismo has seven breeds of donkey from the Apulian *asino gigante* to the Ragusa donkey for riding, stroking and admiring. *4 rooms | Contrada Piano Milo | Noto | mobile tel. 32 00 98 04 24 | www.agrimilo.it | Budget–Moderate*

THE NORTH COAST

INSIDER TIP ▶ CAVE DWELLINGS AND SPERLINGA CASTLE (139 F3) *(ᗰ H4)*

Some of the caverns under this castle near Nicosia are still lived in today, others are stables and some are readily accessible. There are *guided tours* of the castle which has a museum on the cave dwellings. *Daily 9.30am–12.30pm, 2.30pm–5pm | admission 3 euros, children 2 euros | tel. 09 31 88 14 99*

MARIONETTE THEATRE IN PALERMO ●

(138 B1) *(ᗰ E3)*
Mimmo Cuticchio (Via Bara all'Olivella 52 | tel. 0 91 32 34 00 | www.figlidartecuticchio. com); Teatro Argento (Via P. Novelli 3 | tel. 09 16 11 36 80 | www.palazzoasmundo. com) and the theatre in the *Museo Internazionale delle Marionette (Piazzetta Niscemi 5 | tel. 0 91 32 80 60)*
Apart form epics, Sicilian tales of knights of old are performed in marionette theatres *(opera* or *teatri dei pupi)*. These in-

clude Charlemagne's struggle against the Saracens or the wooing of the beautiful Angelica which always involve a lot of action and the clinking of swords.

MARIONETTE THEATRE IN SIRACUSA
● (143 E4) (𝄞 L7)

Emancipated princesses and dragon slayers take to the stage at the delightful theatre run by the *Vaccaro-Mauceri families (Via Giudecca 17/19 and 22 | Piazza S. Giuseppe 33 | tel. 09 31 46 55 40 | www.pupari.com)* with performances held almost every day from March to October (children under 3 free, concessions for children under 10). Visitors can also see these intricate, handmade puppets in the *laboratorio* (puppet workshop) and the *museum (Mon–Sat 10.30am/11am–1pm and 5pm–7.30pm (in the winter 3–5pm).*

PALERMO CALCIO STORE
(138 B1) (𝄞 E3)

Kit out your *bambini* in the colours of the only Sicilian football club playing in the professional league. The pink kit (in memory of the city's patron saint, Saint Rosalia) also suits girls. Or why not buy the pink and black football as the ultimate souvenir to show off? *Via Maqueda 397*

THE SOUTHWEST

TRAPANI SALT WORKS
(136 C3) (𝄞 C4)

In the middle of the salt pans near Trapani there is an old windmill that has been converted into a museum. Visitors can see how the salt water was pumped from one evaporation basin to the next before electricity was invented, and how the boulders of crystallised salt are ground. Canoes are available for hire. There are boat trips around Mozia lagoon and to the islands in the shallow sea *Stagno di Marsala* where you can also do some birdwatching (e.g. flamingos and avocets). *Daily 9.30am–7pm | Paceco, Contrada Nubia | free admission | www. wwfsalineditrapani.it | www.museodelo sale.it*

Let your dreams fly high: Sicily's child-friendly beaches and the deep-blue sea

FESTIVALS & EVENTS

Most Sicilian festivals have a religious origin. The most important annual event is Holy Week, *settimana santa*: Many towns stage moving processions with mournful music, passion plays and colourful wooden figurines. Other highlights include the feasts of the patron saints and *carnevale*, celebrated in some towns on the island.

FESTIVALS & EVENTS

3–5 FEBRUARY
Sant'Agata in Catania – feast of the patron saint at the foot of the Etna

FEBRUARY/MARCH
Almond blossom festival in Agrigento in the Valle dei Templi – with parades of marching bands
Carnival processions in Sciacca and Acireale with masks and carts

MAUNDY THURSDAY
Veronica procession in Marsala

GOOD FRIDAY
Procession of penitents in Trapani – with hundreds of hooded men and children
INSIDER TIP ▶ *I Giudei* in San Fratello – a burlesque-aggressive folk festival

EASTER
The Dance of the Devils in Prizzi – garish spectacle to chase out the winter
Albanian processions and dances in Piana degli Albanesi

2ND HALF OF APRIL
Street Food Fest in Palermo – food trucks and stalls offer snacks such as *arancine* or *pulpo*. www.palermo streetfoodfest.it

AROUND 10 MAY
Sant'Alfio in Trecastagni – folklore and parade of sicilian carts

3RD SUNDAY IN MAY
Infiorata in Noto – the stairways in this Baroque town are decorated in designs made entirely of flower petals

MAY–JUNE
Greek Theatre Festival in Syracuse – performances of ancient tragedies where they were once performed 2500 years ago. www.indafondazione.org

14/15 JULY
U Fistinu in Palermo – festival of Santa Roalia, with processions, fair and concerts

The Dance of the Devils and carnival festivities: the Sicilians celebrate religious festivals with abandon – and lots of colour, noise and fun

MID JULY–SEPTEMBER

Taormina Arte – summer festival in the Greek-roman theatres with modern theatre and classical music performances. One branch of the festival deals with the cinema. *www.taormina-arte.com*

10 AUGUST

San San Sebastiano in Palazzolo Acreide – the saints' procession turns into a confetti battle. *www.sansebastiano.org*

10–15 AUGUST

Mata and Grifone in Messina – with huge figures on horses celebrating the liberation of Sicily from the Arabs

12–14 AUGUST

Palio dei Normanni in Piazza Armerina – stages medieval-themed riding tournaments

MID/LATE SEPTEMBER

INSIDER TIP *Couscous festival* in San Vito Lo Capo, including the couscous world championships. In 2017, the champion was Angola! *www.couscousfest.it*

13 DECEMBER

Santa Lucia in Syracuse – procession and festival of light

NATIONAL HOLIDAYS

1 January	New Year's Day
6 January	Epiphany
13 April 2020, 5 April 2021	
	Easter Monday
25 April	Anniversary of the Liberation from Fascism
1 May	Labour Day
2 June	Founding of the Republic
15 August	Assumption Day
1 November	All Saints' Day
8 December	Immaculate Conception
25 December	Christmas
26 December	Santo Stefano

LINKS, BLOGS, APPS & MORE

www.visitsicily.info Official portal of the Office for Tourism, Sport and Theatre (in English) which also serves as a blog which touches on highly disputed issues such as social responsibility. Appealing photos and up-to-date calendar of events

www.regione.sicilia.it/beniculturali/dirbenicult/musei/museivirtualtour.html Visit more than 20 museums and excavation sites, some have virtual tours that are useful when planning a visit to such huge sites as the Valley of the Temples in Agrigento, for example. Photos, site plans, information in Italian only

travel.nationalgeographic.com/travel/countries/sicily-italy-photos A visual and aesthetic album of atmospheric photographs from the *National Geographic*. Each with an informative caption giving an intimate glimpse of life on Sicily

www.cucinario.it Eating and drinking in Palermo and the whole of Sicily, as well as other regions in Italy. Mouth-watering photos, information in Italian only. Lots of Sicilian recipes that really make you want to get to work in the kitchen – or book a flight to Sicily

www.larosaworks.com/sicily_tours_film_list.php List of films shot in Sicily – from "The Godfather" to "Cinema Paradiso"

www.sicilianplaces.co.uk/blog/ Good blog with lots of information on places

www.walksicily.de/walks.html Information about the best hiking trails on Sicily (in English)

siciliancuisine.blogspot.com Lots of delicious Sicilian recipes, even with step-by-step photos

www.siciliafan.it Sicilians and fellow fans of Sicily share their tips and advice on topics such as folk music, the environment or homesickness

Regardless of whether you are still researching your trip or already in Sicily: these addresses will provide you with more information, videos and networks to make your holiday even more enjoyable

www.siciliarunning.it This website provides a list of marathon dates, running races along the paths of Mount Etna and jogging groups

www.youtube.com/watch?v=3Sum27UCIpA&feature=related Colourful masquerade on Good Friday in San Fratello where the "Red Devils" interrupt the festive procession

www.youtube.com/watch?v=SHx-4P8J3KE8 A trip to Stromboli, Vulcano and Etna – a good first impression of all those active volcanoes on and around Sicily

www.youtube.com/watch?v=Md56FuGgryU Beautiful timelapse vistas of Sicily

www.youtube.com/watch?v=wYq-BtZAYUg&NR=1 English-language video diary by Sara and Ees tracking their European journey. Four entertaining episodes follow their guide as he shows them around Palermo. After an evening meal with their guide and a conversation about the Mafia, they say farewell to Palermo before their journey continues to Tel Aviv

Sicilian Dictionary Amaze the locals with your grasp of the local dialect. This app translator comes up with the appropriate phrase for everyday situations, declarations of love and insults in the Sicilian vernacular

Sicily Beaches The best (or nearest) beaches on the island, listed logically, well illustrated. A must for sun worshippers

Ricette siciliani collana *Pasta alla norma* and *cassata* to make at home: Sicilian recipes including a list of ingredients and degrees of difficulty, in Italian/English/French

NOma Covers everything about the opposition to the Mafia and businesses who refuse to pay protection money

WineCode Sicilia A guide from the Istituto Regionale for Wine and Oil listing the most interesting wineries (in English)

TRAVEL TIPS

ARRIVAL

Although it can take forever to drive down through Italy, the journey by motorway offers spectacular sights. The mountain highway running from Salerno to Reggio di Calabria has finally opened after years of construction work. Alternatives are the car ferries Genoa–Palermo, Civitavecchia–Termini Imerese and Naples–Palermo. Prices, timetables and reservations under *www.traghetti.com* and *www.gnv.it*

Travelling by train from the UK involves several changes – in Italy, either in Milan or Rome. There are no direct lines through Europe. The cost of a sleeper and supplements for Inter City trains usually make the journey more expensive than flying. *www.trenitalia.it*

A number of different airlines fly from the UK and Ireland directly to Sicily

(usually Palermo or Catania). These include British Airways, Ryanair, easyJet, BMI Baby, Thomson and Aer Lingus. Sicily is also well connected to many airports on the Italian mainland with Alitalia. Direct buses run from the airport in Catania *(www.aeroporto.catania.it)* to Messina, Taormina, Ragusa, Enna, Cefalù, Agrigento and Syracuse; from Palermo airport *(www.gesap.it)* to Trapani. There's also an airport in Trapani *(www.airgest.it)*. The new Comiso airport in the southeast is so far only connected to London-Stansted, Dublin and Brussels (Ryanair) *(www.aeroportodicomiso.eu)*.

CAMPING

There are around 100 campsites on Sicily and the nearby islands. Most are on the sea and are open between Easter and the end of Oct *(www.camping.it)*. In addition, there are hundreds of places for staying overnight in your motorhome, e.g. carparks at beaches that are often free but have no facilities. There are also a few sites for motorhomes with washing facilities, roofs for shade and trees.

CAR HIRE

Major car rental companies can be found in Palermo, Catania, Syracuse, Messina, Taormina and at the airports. Prices are from around 185 euros per week if you book on the Internet outside Italy. Booking locally costs around 25% more.

COOKERY CLASSES

 Sicilian cooking is booming as are the cooking courses available. One popular

RESPONSIBLE TRAVEL

It doesn't take a lot to be environmentally friendly whilst travelling. Don't just think about your carbon footprint whilst flying to and from your holiday destination but also about how you can protect nature and culture abroad. As a tourist it is especially important to respect nature, look out for local products, cycle instead of driving, save water and much more. If you would like to find out more about eco-tourism please visit: *www.ecotourism.org*

website offering a wide range of cooking classes and courses for everyone's tastes and abilities is *www.annatascalanza.com*. The *padrona* of *Agriturismo San Leonardello (Via Madonna della Libertà 165 | tel. 0 95 96 40 20 | www.san leonardello.it)* in Giarre reveals how to get the hole in the *maccheroni*. Those interested in learning the secrets behind the world-renowned *pasticceria siciliana* can take part in the cannoli cooking class organised by *Pasticceria d'Amore* (see p. 44) in Taormina.

CUSTOMS

There are no longer any allowance restrictions for EU citizens on tax-free items. If you are arriving from a non-EU country, different regulations apply. Check the Internet before leaving home. For tax and duty on goods brought to the UK see: *www.gov.uk/uk-border-control*

DRIVING

The maximum speed in built-up areas is 50 km/h (30 mph), on main roads 90 km/h (55 mph), on dual carriageways 110 km/h (66 mph), and 130 km/h (80 mph) on motorways (110 km/h/66 mph in the rain; 50 km/h/30 mph in fog). Seatbelts must be worn on all seats. It is mandatory to drive with dipped headlights outside built-up areas during the day. There must be an emergency jacket in the car. It is recommended taking a Green Card insurance document with you. The blood alcohol concentration limit is 0.5mg/ alcohol per 100 ml/blood. If you get caught, you'll pay for all those who slip through the net. Speeding offences of-

CURRENCY CONVERTER

£	€	€	£
1	1.15	1	0.87
3	3.45	3	2.61
5	5.74	5	4.35
13	14.93	13	11.32
40	46	40	35
75	86	75	65
120	138	120	104
250	287	250	218
500	574	500	435

$	€	€	$
1	0.88	1	1.13
3	2.64	3	3.40
5	4.41	5	5.67
13	11.46	13	14.75
40	35	40	45
75	66	75	85
120	106	120	136
250	220	250	284
500	441	500	567

For current exchange rates see www.xe.com

more than 40km/h (25mph) and drunken driving (more than 1.5mg/alcohol per 100ml/blood) will cost you between 1500–6000 euros, your licence and the car that is then auctioned off. This also applies to non-Italians and for hire cars too!

In many places, no-parking zones are only marked with coloured lines on the edge of the pavement. No markings means unrestricted parking, unless signs tell you something else; yellow means reserved for the police, the *carabinieri* and local buses; black and yellow means no parking; blue means pay-and-display. Tickets can usually be bought in bars, shops, kiosks. You have to scratch the respective fields to show the time and date.

ELECTRICITY

220 Volts. Only flat pin plugs fit, otherwise an adapter is needed. International plug adapters are often not compatible!

EMBASSIES & CONSULATES

BRITISH EMBASSY
Via XX Settembre 80/a | 00187 Rome | tel. +39 06 4220 0001 | www.gov.uk/world/ organisations/british-embassy-rome

US CONSULATE GENERAL
Piazza della Repubblica | 80122 Napoli | tel. +39 081 583 8111 | it.usembassy.gov/ embassy-consulates/naples/

EMBASSY OF CANADA
Via Zara 30 | 00198 Rome | tel. +39 06 85444 2911 | www.canada.it

EMERGENCY SERVICES

Accident/police: tel. 112 and 113 | Breakdown assistance: mobile tel. 8 00 11 68 00 or tel. 03 92 10 41 | Ambulance: tel. 118 | Fire brigade and forest fires: tel. 115 and 1515 | Coast guard: tel. 1530

ENTRANCE FEES

Most state museums and historic/excavation sites cost between 4 and 14 euros; EU citizens under 18 have free admission, youths between 18–25 are entitled to a 25–50 % discount (1st Sunday of the month free). Entrance is free to many small museums, but donations are welcome. Custodians who unlock churches and palaces should be given a tip of around 5 euros.

FARM HOLIDAYS/ AGRITOURISM

Holidaying on a farm has become a popular, low-cost and child-friendly concept throughout Italy, and gives visitors a chance to get to know an area and the people better. Agritourism on Sicily with its feudal structure often means staying in historic country houses – where the atmosphere in "The Leopard" is brought back to life. Many farms have mountainbikes and/or horses and organise excursions. Virtually all *agriturismi* serve good country food – after all, they have to produce their own food to be certified. Information under *www.agriturismosicilia.it*

HEALTH

The least complicated method: in case of illness, pay for your doctor and medicine on the spot and present your bills to the health service when you return home for problem-free reimbursement. The European Health Insurance Card (EHC) is also accepted. Emergency treatment in public hospitals is no longer entirely free of charge. X-rays and other diagnostic services incur charges which have to be paid directly to the hospital. Further information under *www.fitfor travel.nhs.uk*

HOTELS

The star categories (one for simple, five for luxury) only give a vague idea of facilities and prices. Tourist information offices have free lists with detailed descriptions of hotels, campsites and private rooms. Prices of rooms must be shown in a room or at the reception desk. They can vary greatly depending on the season.

IMMIGRATION

Visas are not reqired for EU citizens; citizens of the US or Canada require a visa only if staying for longer than three months. Only rarely do passports need to be shown at airports, but are required when checking into hotels and campsites.

INFORMATION IN ADVANCE

ITALIAN STATE TOURIST BOARD (ENIT)
1, Princes Street | London W1B 2AY | tel. +44 20 74 08 12 54 | www.enit.it | e-mail: info.london@enit.it.

INFORMATION IN SICILY

The 23 offices run by the *Servizio Turistico Regionale (STR)* can be found in 9 privincial capitals and in 14 major holiday centres. For more information see: *www.pti. regione.sicilia.it.* All STR offices can be contacted by e-mail according to thispattern: *strcefalu@regione.sicilia.it.*
Young people can usually speak English. When there is no STR or other information centre, try a travel agent or the local police *(polizia municipale or vigili urbani)*, who are generally very helpful. Most hotels and guesthouses also have maps and leaflets. Almost all communes have very informative websites with further links. For general information on Sicily, see: *www.regione.sicilia.it/turismo*
Information on state museums and excavation sites can also be found online: *www.regione.sicilia.it/beniculturali.*

OPENING HOURS

Shops, supermarkets and department stores are generally open from 8.30am–1pm and 4/5pm–8pm. Shops close one afternoon a week – this varies however from shop to shop. During the high season, most shops in tourist areas are open all day and some well into the night. Garages are often closed on Sundays and after 8pm.

PHONE & MOBILE PHONE

There are not many public phones boxes anymore. Most of them accept coins; telephone cards can be purchased in post

BUDGETING

Tomatoes	£0.87/$1.14– £8.70/$11.35	*for 1 kg in summer, depending on the variety*
Coffee	from £0.70/$0.90	*for an espresso*
Wine	£2.60/$3.40– £5.20/$6.80	*for a carafe of wine (¼ litre)*
Petrol	£1.26/$1.65– £1.39/$1.82	*for 1 litre of super*
Coppola	approx. £44/$57	*for a designer cap*
Buses in towns	£1.04/$1.36– £1.39/$1.82	*per trip*

offices, newsagents and *tabacchi*. Long-distance calls are always possible without restrictions. A local call from a public phone (43 sec) costs 10–20 cents; a 3-min. call abroad (to the UK) approx. 5 euros. Service numbers (code 800) of tourist bureaux and hotels are free.
The mobile phone is called *cellulare* or *telefonino* in Italian. If you intend phoning a lot within Italy, an Italian SIM card is worth it. These can be bought in any

phone shop, even if you have no Italian tax no. *(codice fiscale)*. A photocopy of your passport is needed.

The country code for Italy is 0039. It is necessary to dial the 0 at the beginning of each fixed-line connection – both from abroad and when making local calls.

POST

Stamps *(francobolli)* are available from post offices, more seldom from tobacconists *(tabacchi)*. Letters and postcards by *posta prioritaria* within Italy cost 95 cents and 1 euro for elsewhere within Europe.

PRICES & CURRENCY

Sicily is not an expensive tourist destination compared to other areas in Italy. An espresso drunk standing in a bar costs less than 1 euro virtually everywhere, a glass of mineral water 50 cents, a beer or an aperitif 2–4 euros. In popular tourist centres, being seated and served at a table can cost two or three times as much. You must budget for between 20–40 euros for a full meal (fish is rather expensive) – but even if you splash out the bill will seldom be for more than 60 euros.

Cash dispensers *(bancomat, postamat)* for withdrawing money with your EC card can also be found in small villages off the beaten track. Not all hotels, restaurants, garages and shops take credit cards. Mastercard and Visa are widely accepted on Sicily; using your EC card with your PIN is less common.

PUBLIC TRANSPORT

Sicily's railway network is not close-knit and mostly single track. IC and express trains often run late and many stations are some way from the village or town centre. An extensive local and regional bus network, operated by a host of private companies, supplements and/or replaces the lack of a good railway system. In many towns, however, there is no central bus station. For more information see: *www.anavsicilia.it*

SMOKING

With very few exceptions, smoking is prohibited in public buildings, restaurants and bars. But as Sicilians like to have an espresso and cigarette standing, they step outside and generally accept this regulation without much complaining. Non-compliance is liable to a fine.

(SUN)BATHING

Carefully laid out sunbeds, such in the *stabilimenti* on the Adriatic, are more typical of the beaches around Taormina. Otherwise sunbathing on Sicily is a pretty relaxed affair and up to each individual. The price of sunshades *(ombrello)* and sunbeds *(lettino, sdraio)* to rent are reasonable by Italian standards. Even though many Sicilian women prefer to go topless and nude bathing is accepted at many beaches such as Torre Salsa near Siculiana, the only official nudist beach (since 2016) is Bulala at Gela.

TAXI

In the large urban centres on Sicily taxis have taximeters. A tip of between 5–10% is usual. In small villages and in the countryside you are best advised to agree on a price with the driver before setting off.

TOILETS

Public WCs are few and far between and not usually in good condition. It is quite normal to drink a quick espresso before using the *bagno* in a bar – in an emergency you can simply place a *mancia* of 50 cents on the bar. *Signore* is the plural of *signora*; a *signore* goes to the gents marked *Signori!*

WEATHER, WHEN TO GO

On the coast, the Mediterannean climate promises long, hot, dry summers. The best months to travel are May, June, September and October when the temperatures are pleasant, the sea warm and you miss the mass invasion of tourists in the high season and the Easter week. The winters are mild and wet. Inland and in the mountains it can be pretty chilly in summer above 1500 m (5000 ft) and snow falls in winter. *www.tempoitalia.it*

WOMEN TRAVELLING SOLO

Until recently, women travelling solo were considered fair game. But even Sicily has entered the modern age, things have become more relaxed and the beach *papagalli* less persistent. Hosts of compliments and flirting however are still very much part of everyday life. It is not necessarily a good idea for women travelling alone to hitch-hike.

WEATHER IN CATANIA

	Jan	Feb	March	April	May	June	July	Aug	Sept	Oct	Nov	Dec
Daytime temperatures in °C/ °F												
	14/57	15/59	17/63	19/66	23/73	28/82	31/88	31/88	28/82	23/73	19/66	16/61
Nighttime temperatures in °C/°F												
	8/46	8/46	9/48	12/54	15/59	19/66	22/72	23/73	20/68	16/61	13/55	9/48
☀	4	5	6	7	8	10	11	10	8	7	6	4
☂	9	5	6	4	3	2	1	1	3	7	7	8
≈	15/59	14/57	14/57	15/59	17/63	21/70	24/75	25/77	24/75	22/72	19/66	16/61

USEFUL PHRASES
ITALIAN

PRONUNCIATION

c, cc	before e or i like ch in "church", e.g. ciabatta, otherwise like k
ch, cch	like k, e.g. pacchi, che
g, gg	before e or i like j in "just", e.g. gente, otherwise like g in "get"
gl	like "lli" in "million", e.g. figlio
gn	as in "cognac", e.g. bagno
sc	before e or i like sh, e.g. uscita
sch	like sk in "skill", e.g. Ischia
z	at the beginning of a word like dz in "adze", otherwise like ts

An accent on an Italian word shows that the stress is on the last syllable.
In other cases we have shown which syllable is stressed by placing a dot below
the relevant vowel.

IN BRIEF

Yes/No/Maybe	Sì/No/Forse
Please/Thank you	Per favore/Grazie
Excuse me, please!	Scusa!/Mi scusi
May I...?/Pardon?	Posso...? / Come dice?/Prego?
I would like to.../Have you got...?	Vorrei.../Avete...?
How much is...?	Quanto costa...?
I (don't) like that	(Non) mi piace
good/bad	buono/cattivo/bene/male
broken/doesn't work	guasto/non funziona
too much/much/little/all/nothing	troppo/molto/poco/tutto/niente
Help!/Attention!/Caution!	aiuto!/attenzione!/prudenza!
ambulance/police/fire brigade	ambulanza/polizia/vigili del fuoco
Prohibition/forbidden/danger/dangerous	divieto/vietato/pericolo/pericoloso
May I take a photo here/of you?	Posso fotografar La?

GREETINGS, FAREWELL

Good morning!/afternoon!/ evening!/night!	Buon giorno!/Buon giorno!/ Buona sera!/Buona notte!
Hello! / Goodbye!/See you	Ciao!/Salve! / Arrivederci!/Ciao!
My name is...	Mi chiamo...
What's your name?	Come si chiama?/Come ti chiami
I'm from...	Vengo da...

Parli italiano?

"Do you speak Italian?" This guide will help you to say the basic words and phrases in Italian.

DATE & TIME

Monday/Tuesday/Wednesday	lunedì/martedì/mercoledì
Thursday/Friday/Saturday	giovedì/venerdì/sabato
Sunday/holiday/ working day	domenica/(giorno) festivo/ (giorno) feriale
today/tomorrow/yesterday	oggi/domani/ieri
hour/minute	ora/minuto
day/night/week/month/year	giorno/notte/settimana/mese/anno
What time is it?	Che ora è? Che ore sono?
It's three o'clock/It's half past three	Sono le tre/Sono le tre e mezza
a quarter to four	le quattro meno un quarto/ un quarto alle quattro

TRAVEL

open/closed	aperto/chiuso
entrance/exit	entrata/uscita
departure/arrival	partenza/arrivo
toilets/ladies/gentlemen	bagno/toilette/signore/signori
(no) drinking water	acqua (non) potabile
Where is...?/Where are...?	Dov'è...?/Dove sono...?
left/right/straight ahead/back	sinistra/destra/dritto/indietro
close/far	vicino/lontano
bus/tram	bus/tram
taxi/cab	taxi/tassì
bus stop/cab stand	fermata/posteggio taxi
parking lot/parking garage	parcheggio/parcheggio coperto
street map/map	pianta/mappa
train station/harbour	stazione/porto
airport	aeroporto
schedule/ticket	orario/biglietto
supplement	supplemento
single/return	solo andata/andata e ritorno
train/track	treno/binario
platform	banchina/binario
I would like to rent...	Vorrei noleggiare...
a car/a bicycle	una macchina/una bicicletta
a boat	una barca
petrol/gas station	distributore/stazione di servizio
petrol/gas / diesel	benzina/diesel/gasolio
breakdown/repair shop	guasto/officina

FOOD & DRINK

Could you please book a table for tonight for four?	Vorrei prenotare per stasera un tavolo per quattro?
on the terrace/by the window	sulla terrazza/ vicino alla finestra
The menu, please	La carta/il menù, per favore
Could I please have...?	Potrei avere...?
bottle/carafe/glass	bottiglia/caraffa/bicchiere
knife/fork/spoon/salt/pepper	coltello/forchetta/cucchiaio/sale/pepe
sugar/vinegar/oil/milk/cream/lemon	zucchero/aceto/olio/latte/panna/limone
cold/too salty/not cooked	freddo/troppo salato/non cotto
with/without ice/sparkling	con/senza ghiaccio/gas
vegetarian/allergy	vegetariano/vegetariana/allergia
May I have the bill, please?	Vorrei pagare/Il conto, per favore
bill/tip	conto/mancia

SHOPPING

Where can I find...?	Dove posso trovare...?
I'd like.../I'm looking for...	Vorrei.../Cerco...
Do you put photos onto CD?	Vorrei masterizzare delle foto su CD?
pharmacy/shopping centre/kiosk	farmacia/centro commerciale/edicola
department store/supermarket	grandemagazzino/supermercato
baker/market/grocery	forno/ mercato/negozio alimentare
photographic items/newspaper shop/	articoli per foto/giornalaio
100 grammes/1 kilo	un etto/un chilo
expensive/cheap/price/more/less	caro/economico/prezzo/di più/di meno
organically grown	di agricoltura biologica

ACCOMMODATION

I have booked a room	Ho prenotato una camera
Do you have any... left?	Avete ancora...
single room/double room	una (camera) singola/doppia
breakfast/half board/	prima colazione/mezza pensione/
full board (American plan)	pensione completa
at the front/seafront/lakefront	con vista/con vista sul mare/lago
shower/sit-down bath/balcony/terrace	doccia/bagno/balcone/terrazza
key/room card	chiave/scheda magnetica
luggage/suitcase/bag	bagaglio/valigia/borsa

BANKS, MONEY & CREDIT CARDS

bank/ATM/pin code	banca/bancomat/ codice segreto
cash/credit card	in contanti/carta di credito
bill/coin/change	banconota/moneta/il resto

HEALTH

doctor/dentist/paediatrician	medico/dentista/pediatra
hospital/emergency clinic	ospedale/pronto soccorso/guardia medica
fever/pain/inflamed/injured	febbre/dolori/infiammato/ferito
diarrhoea/nausea/sunburn	diarrea/nausea/scottatura solare
plaster/bandage/ointment/cream	cerotto/fasciatura/pomata/crema
pain reliever/tablet/suppository	antidolorifico/compressa/supposta

POST, TELECOMMUNICATIONS & MEDIA

stamp/letter/postcard	francobollo/lettera/cartolina
I need a landline phone card/	Mi serve una scheda telefonica per la
I'm looking for a prepaid card for my	rete fissa/Cerco una scheda prepagata
mobile	per il mio cellulare
Where can I find internet access?	Dove trovo un accesso internet?
dial/connection/engaged	comporre/linea/occupato
socket/adapter/charger	presa/riduttore/caricabatterie
computer/battery/rechargeable battery	computer/batteria/accumulatore
internet address (URL)/e-mail address	indirizzo internet/indirizzo email
internet connection/wifi	collegamento internet/wi-fi
e-mail/file/print	email/file/stampare

LEISURE, SPORTS & BEACH

beach/bathing beach	spiaggia/bagno/stabilimento balneare
sunshade/lounger/cable car/chair lift	ombrellone/sdraio/funivia/seggiovia
(rescue) hut/avalanche	rifugio/valanga

NUMBERS

0	zero	15	quindici
1	uno	16	sedici
2	due	17	diciassette
3	tre	18	diciotto
4	quattro	19	diciannove
5	cinque	20	venti
6	sei	21	ventuno
7	sette	50	cinquanta
8	otto	100	cento
9	nove	200	duecento
10	dieci	1000	mille
11	undici	2000	duemila
12	dodici	10000	diecimila
13	tredici	½	un mezzo
14	quattordici	¼	un quarto

ROAD ATLAS

The green line indicates the Discovery Tour "Sicily at a glance"
The blue line indicates the other Discovery Tours

All tours are also marked on the pull-out map

Photo: "Temple E" in Selinunte

Exploring Sicily

The map on the back cover shows how the area has been sub-divided

A   **B**

1

Mare

Isola di Ustica
Ustica

M e d i t e r r a n e o

Napoli

de

2

Tonnara
di Bonagia

⭐**13**

Trapani   **Erice**   **Va**

14

Isole Egadi   *Isola di Levanzo*   113   12

Isola
Formica   **Paceco**

Tunis   Levanzo   *Isola*
Maraone   Nubia   9   8

3   686   Marettimo   *Via del Sale*   6

Isola
Marettimo   314 ▲ Favignana   Marausa   Marsala
Marausa

②   Birgi   **31**

Isola Favignana   ✈ TPS   ▲ San   Mend

Isole dello
Stagnone   Pantaleo   22   30
Mozia   Pozzillo   ⊤

17   S. Filippo   21
e Giacomo

Marsala   115

Capo Boeo   188   Ciavolo
o Lilibeo

10

4   Lido
Signorino   Strasatti   Borga
Costie

Pizzolato   ①   115   **42**
11   Mazara d.V.

Mazara
del Vallo

5   Granitola
Torrett

C
a
n
a
l
e

d
i

S
i
c
i
l

Pantelleria

6
10 km
6.2 mi

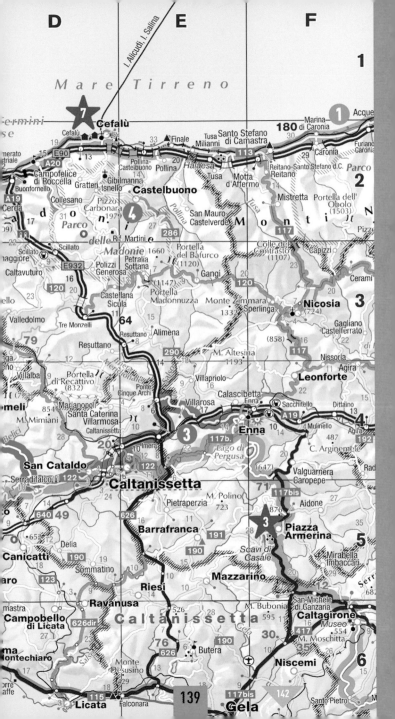

KEY TO ROAD ATLAS

Autobahn mit Anschlussstellen
Motorway with junctions

Autobahn in Bau
Motorway under construction

Mautstelle
Toll station

Raststätte mit Übernachtung
Roadside restaurant and hotel

Raststätte
Roadside restaurant

Tankstelle
Filling-station

Autobahnähnliche Schnell-
straße mit Anschlussstelle
Dual carriage-way with
motorway characteristics
with junction

Fernverkehrsstraße
Trunk road

Durchgangsstraße
Thoroughfare

Wichtige Hauptstraße
Important main road

Hauptstraße
Main road

Nebenstraße
Secondary road

Eisenbahn
Railway

Autozug-Terminal
Car-loading terminal

Zahnradbahn
Mountain railway

Kabinenschwebebahn
Aerial cableway

Eisenbahnfähre
Railway ferry

Autofähre
Car ferry

Schifffahrtslinie
Shipping route

Landschaftlich besonders
schöne Strecke
Route with
beautiful scenery

Alleenstr. Touristenstraße
Tourist route

XI-V Wintersperre
Closure in winter

Straße für Kfz gesperrt
Road closed to motor traffic

8% Bedeutende Steigungen
Important gradients

Für Wohnwagen nicht
empfehlenswert
Not recommended
for caravans

Für Wohnwagen gesperrt
Closed for caravans

Besonders schöner Ausblick
Important panoramic view

* *Wartenstein* Sehenswert: Kultur - Natur
* *Umbalfälle* Of interest: culture - nature

Badestrand
Bathing beach

Nationalpark, Naturpark
National park, nature park

Sperrgebiet
Prohibited area

Kirche
Church

Kloster
Monastery

Schloss, Burg
Palace, castle

Moschee
Mosque

Ruinen
Ruins

Leuchtturm
Lighthouse

Turm
Tower

Höhle
Cave

Ausgrabungsstätte
Archaeological excavation

Jugendherberge
Youth hostel

Allein stehendes Hotel
Isolated hotel

Berghütte
Refuge

Campingplatz
Camping site

Flughafen
Airport

Regionalflughafen
Regional airport

Flugplatz
Airfield

Staatsgrenze
National boundary

Verwaltungsgrenze
Administrative boundary

Grenzkontrollstelle
Check-point

Grenzkontrollstelle mit
Beschränkung
Check-point with
restrictions

ROMA Hauptstadt
Capital

VENEZIA Verwaltungssitz
Seat of the administration

MARCO POLO Erlebnistour 1
MARCO POLO Discovery Tour 1

MARCO POLO Erlebnistouren
MARCO POLO Discovery Tours

MARCO POLO Highlight
MARCO POLO Highlight

FOR YOUR NEXT TRIP...

MARCO POLO TRAVEL GUIDES

Travel with
Insider Tips

INDEX

This index lists all places, sights and beaches in this guide.
Numbers in bold indicate a main entry.

WRITE TO US

e-mail: info@marcopologuides.co.uk

Did you have a great holiday?
Is there something on your mind?
Whatever it is, let us know!
Whether you want to praise, alert us to errors or give us a personal tip –
MARCO POLO would be pleased to hear from you.
We do everything we can to provide the very latest information for your trip.

Nevertheless, despite all of our authors' thorough research, errors can creep in. MARCO POLO does not accept any liability for this. Please contact us by e-mail or post.

MARCO POLO Travel Publishing Ltd
Pinewood, Chineham Business Park
Crockford Lane, Chineham
Basingstoke, Hampshire RG24 8AL
United Kingdom

PICTURE CREDITS
Cover photograph: Cala Tonnarella dell'Uzzo (Schapowalow/SIME: A. Bartuccio)
Photographs: Agriturismo Limoneto: Dora Moscati (19 top); DuMont Bildarchiv: Feldhoff/Martin (38, 39, 52, 62, 85, 120/121), S. Lubenow (25); F. M. Frei (10); R. Freyer (5, 30/31, 37, 41, 51, 58, 65); R. Hackenberg (4 bottom, 72/73, 81, 115, 134/135); huber-images: A. Bartuccio (29, 46/47, 57, 60/61, 96/97), M. Carassale (67), G. Cozzi (69), Gräfenhain (54, 101), Liese (flap left, 74), L. Linder (31), Lubenow (7), M. Ripani (78), Saffo (14/15), A. Saffo (2, 17, 34, 45), Simeone (4 top, 12/13); huber-images/SIME: Saffo (8, 111); Kempinski Hotel Giardino di Costanza: Adrian Huston (18 centre); M. Kirchgessner (26/27, 28 right, 30, 42/43, 77, 86/87, 112/113, 120, 121, 122 bottom); La Terra Magica: Lenz (flap right, 32/33, 88, 90, 93); Laif: Barbagallo (6), Celentano (19 bottom, 122 top), Madej (123); Laif/Contrasto: Shobha (11); Laif/Le Figaro Magazine: S. Frances (83), Martin (18 top); mauritius images cubolmages (106); mauritius images/Alamy (104); mauritius images/Cubolmages (9); mauritius images/Cubolmages (48, 71); mauritius images/foodcollection (28 left); mauritius images/imagebroker: Bahnmüller (20/21); mauritius images/Rubberball (3); mauritius images/United Archives (107); Paradise Beach Club (18 bottom); picture alliance: D. Parra Saiani (23); Schapowalow/SIME: A. Bartuccio (1); T. Stankiewicz (95, 119); vario images: Baumgarten (116/117)

3rd Edition – fully revised and updated 2020
Worldwide Distribution: Marco Polo Travel Publishing Ltd, Pinewood, Chineham Business Park, Crockford Lane, Basingstoke, Hampshire RG24 8AL, United Kingdom. Email: sales@marcopolouk.com
© MAIRDUMONT GmbH & Co. KG, Ostfildern
Chief editor: Stefanie Penck; Author: Hans Bausenhardt, co-author: Peter Peter, editor: Arnd M. Schuppius
Programme supervision: Lucas Forst-Gill, Susanne Heimburger, Tamara Hub, Johanna Jiranek, Nikolai Michaelis, Kristin Wittemann, Tim Wohlbold; Picture editor: Gabriele Forst; What's hot: Peter Peter; wunder media, Munich
Cartography road atlas & pull-out map: © MAIRDUMONT, Ostfildern
Design front cover, p. 1, pull-out map cover: Karl Anders – Büro für Visual Stories, Hamburg; interior: milchhot:atelier, Berlin; Discovery Tours, p. 2/3: Susan Chaaban Dipl.-Des. (FH)
Translated from German by Susan Jones, Christopher Wynne
Prepress: writehouse, Cologne; InterMedia, Ratingen
Phrase book in cooperation with Ernst Klett Sprachen GmbH, Stuttgart, Editorial by Pons Wörterbücher

MIX
Paper from responsible sources
FSC® C124385

DOS & DON'TS ☝

A few things you should bear in mind when on Sicily

DON'T DRIVE INTO THE CITY

For some, the ultimate kick for others a nerve-racking experience. Driving in the cities of Palermo and Catania with the constant beeping of horns, hair-raising takeover manoeuvres, pot holes and not a parking space in sight is nothing for the faint-hearted.

DO TRY THE LOCAL SPECIALITIES

Almost all restaurants have a set-meal – the *menú turistico* – at a price that includes two courses, a dessert, a drink, the cover charge, tax and service. Very few locals ever choose this even though it is much cheaper than eating à la carte. The food is generally pretty uninspiring and only very seldom are typical local dishes served.

DON'T GO AROUND TOWN TOPLESS

Sicily appears to be a laid-back place but the basic rules of etiquette and decency still apply. Although increasingly more women go topless on beaches, the body must not be exposed to view in towns or at the beach trattoria, and this goes for men too. At the end of the day, Sicily is not a 24x7 party island.

DON'T PLAY WITH FIRE

Year after year hundreds of fires destroy woods, olive groves and gardens, and threaten houses and even whole villages. Usually only a barren stone desert is left afterwards. Cigarette butts, picnic fires, the hot exhaust of your car parked on dry grass or leaves can all have catastrophic consequences.

DON'T INVITE THIEVES

Thieves and pickpockets are not lurking on every corner but there is a greater risk in the larger cities, ports and on a number of beaches. Don't leave anything visible in a car or else you risk having the windows smashed. When driving through Palermo and Catania lock the doors and the boot. Thefts from cars on Sicily are not generally worse than anywhere else, but these two cities appear quite near the top of the statistics table for robbery in Italy. This applies especially to handbag thefts from moving cars and mopeds *(scippo)*. Don't carry a handbag or shoulder bag unless you really have to.

DO TIP GENEROUSLY

In virtually no other region in Europe do people tip as generously as in Sicily – the average is 10 percent. Locals are only too aware of the precarious situation of the staff working there who are not always paid the basic wage. The same applies at the bar: place a coin on your receipt *(scontrino)* and you will be rewarded with a smile and will probably be served faster.